Favorite Brand Name

GREAT–TASTING
POTATOES

GREAT
Beginnings

Potatoes can add a special touch to an appetizer buffet. Surprise your guests with stuffed new potatoes, homemade herbed chips or spicy potato skins.

Cheesy Potato Skins
with Black Beans & Salsa ▶

6 medium potatoes (6 ounces each), baked
¾ cup GUILTLESS GOURMET® Black Bean Dip (mild or spicy)
¾ cup GUILTLESS GOURMET® Nacho Dip (mild or spicy)

¾ cup GUILTLESS GOURMET® Salsa (mild, medium or hot)
¾ cup low fat sour cream
Fresh cilantro sprigs (optional)

Preheat oven to 400°F. Cut baked potatoes in half lengthwise and scoop out potato pulp, leaving ¼-inch pulp attached to skin (avoid breaking skin). Save potato pulp for another use, such as mashed potatoes. Place potato skins on large baking sheet, skin sides down; bake 5 minutes.

Fill each potato skin with 1 tablespoon bean dip and 1 tablespoon nacho dip. Return to oven; bake 10 minutes. Remove from oven; let cool 5 minutes. Dollop 1 tablespoon salsa and 1 tablespoon sour cream onto each potato. Garnish with cilantro, if desired. Serve hot.   *Makes 12 servings*

Nutrients per serving *(1 potato skin): Calories: 133, Total Fat: 1 g, Saturated Fat: 0 g, Cholesterol: 5 mg, Sodium: 216 mg, Protein: 4 g, Dietary Fiber: 3 g*

Southern Stuffed New Potatoes with Wisconsin Asiago, Ham and Mushrooms ▼

12 small new red-skinned
   potatoes (1½ to 2 inches
   diameter)
2 tablespoons Wisconsin butter,
   melted
1 teaspoon Wisconsin butter
2 ounces cooked ham, chopped
¼ cup chopped onion
1 teaspoon chopped fresh thyme
½ teaspoon finely chopped garlic
4 ounces button mushrooms,
   chopped
2½ ounces portobello mushrooms,
   chopped*

2½ ounces oyster mushrooms,
   stemmed and chopped*
3 tablespoons whipping cream
½ cup (2 ounces) shredded
   Wisconsin Asiago cheese
   Salt
   Black pepper
½ cup (2 ounces) shredded
   Wisconsin baby Swiss cheese
½ cup (2 ounces) shredded
   Wisconsin medium white
   Cheddar cheese
¼ cup chopped fresh parsley

Preheat oven to 400°F. Cut ¼ inch off each end of potatoes; discard ends. Cut potatoes in half crosswise. In large bowl, stir together potatoes and 2 tablespoons melted butter until potatoes are well coated. Place potatoes on parchment-lined 15×10-inch jelly-roll pan. Bake for 30 to 40 minutes or until fork tender. Let cool slightly. Scoop out potato pulp, leaving thin shells. Reserve potato pulp for another use. Set shells aside.

Melt 1 teaspoon butter in large skillet over medium-high heat. Add ham; cook 2 to 5 minutes or just until ham begins to brown, stirring occasionally. Add onion, thyme and garlic; decrease heat to medium-low. Cook and stir 2 to 3 minutes or until onion is tender. Add mushrooms. Cook 5 to 6 minutes or until liquid is evaporated, stirring occasionally. Add whipping cream; cook 1 minute, stirring constantly, or until cream is thickened. Stir in Asiago cheese. Season to taste with salt and pepper.

Remove skillet from heat. Meanwhile, in medium bowl, combine baby Swiss and white Cheddar cheeses; set aside. Fill potato shells with mushroom mixture; sprinkle evenly with Swiss and Cheddar cheese mixture. Cover; refrigerate overnight. To bake, allow potatoes to stand at room temperature for 45 minutes. Preheat oven to 400°F. Bake 12 to 15 minutes or until cheeses are melted and lightly browned. Sprinkle with chopped parsley. *Makes 24 appetizers*

*Substitute 5 ounces button mushrooms for portobello and oyster mushrooms, if desired.

Favorite recipe from **Wisconsin Milk Marketing Board**

Nacho Potato Appetizers

2 Colorado russet variety
   potatoes, cut into ¼-inch
   slices
¼ cup taco sauce
¼ cup roasted red pepper, cut
   into julienne strips
¼ cup pitted black olives, cut into
   wedges

1½ cups (6 ounces) shredded
   Cheddar or Monterey Jack
   cheese
   Cilantro or parsley sprigs
¼ cup sour cream or plain yogurt
½ cup salsa

continued on page 6

Preheat oven to 375°F. Grease shallow baking pan. Arrange potato slices in prepared pan. Brush tops with taco sauce. Bake for 10 minutes or until tender. Top with pepper, olives and cheese. Bake 5 minutes longer or until cheese is melted. Garnish with cilantro. Serve with sour cream and salsa. *Makes 4 servings*

Green Guacamole Nachos: Combine 1 mashed small ripe avocado, ¼ cup softened pimiento-flavored cream cheese, 2 tablespoons chopped green chilies, 1 teaspoon lime juice and ⅛ teaspoon garlic salt. Substitute avocado mixture for peppers, olives and cheese. Bake and serve as directed above.

Nutrients per serving: Calories: 336, Total Fat: 18 g, Cholesterol: 51 mg, Sodium: 602 mg, Protein: 14 g, Dietary Fiber: 3 g

*Favorite recipe from **Colorado Potato Administrative Committee***

Beef & Potato Empanadas

6 ounces cooked roast beef, shredded
½ cup chopped green onion tops
¼ cup finely chopped onion
1 tablespoon canned chopped jalapeño pepper
½ teaspoon bottled minced garlic

½ teaspoon salt
½ teaspoon black pepper
2 medium Colorado potatoes, cooked, peeled and chopped
¼ cup beef broth
2 frozen puff pastry sheets, thawed

To make filling, combine beef, green onions, onion, jalapeño pepper, garlic, salt and black pepper in medium bowl; mix well. Stir in potatoes and enough of the beef broth to moisten and hold mixture together.

Preheat oven to 400°F. Roll out each pastry sheet to 12×12-inch square on lightly floured surface. Cut each square into nine 4-inch squares. Place rounded tablespoonful of filling on each square. Fold over to form triangle; seal edges with fork. Place on baking sheet. Bake about 20 minutes or until golden. *Makes 18 empanadas*

Nutrients per serving (1 empanada): Calories: 146, Total Fat: 8 g, Cholesterol: 6 mg, Sodium: 213 mg, Protein: 5 g, Dietary Fiber: trace

*Favorite recipe from **Colorado Potato Administrative Committee***

Spicy Lamb & Potato Nests

Potato Nests

- 2 unpeeled small Colorado potatoes, shredded
- 1 egg
- 1 tablespoon vegetable oil
- 1 tablespoon grated Parmesan cheese
- ¼ teaspoon garlic powder
- ¼ teaspoon black pepper
- ¼ cup biscuit mix
  Fine, dry bread crumbs

Lamb Filling

- 8 ounces lean ground lamb
- ¼ cup chopped green onion
- 1 teaspoon grated fresh ginger or ¼ teaspoon dry ginger
- ½ teaspoon ground cumin
- ¼ teaspoon salt
- ¼ teaspoon ground coriander
- ¼ teaspoon ground cinnamon
- ¼ teaspoon ground red pepper
- ¼ cup jalapeño pepper jelly

To prepare Potato Nests, place potatoes in medium bowl. Cover with cold water; let stand 5 minutes. Drain well; pat dry with paper towels. Preheat oven to 400°F. Whisk together egg, oil, cheese, garlic powder and black pepper. Stir in biscuit mix until well blended. Stir in shredded potato. Generously grease 16 muffin cups; sprinkle bottom of each lightly with bread crumbs. Spoon about 1 tablespoon of potato mixture into each cup; make slight indentation in center. Bake 15 minutes. Remove from oven and keep warm.

Meanwhile to prepare Lamb Filling, cook and stir lamb and onion in saucepan over medium-high heat until lamb is no longer pink and onion is tender. Drain well; add ginger, cumin, salt, coriander, cinnamon and red pepper. Cook and stir 1 to 2 minutes until flavors are blended. Add jelly; heat until jelly is melted and lamb mixture is heated through. Spoon lamb mixture by rounded teaspoonfuls onto potato nests. Serve hot.

Makes 16 appetizers

Note: Spicy Lamb & Potato Nests may be made ahead, covered and refrigerated. Just before serving wrap in foil and heat in preheated 350°F oven for 10 minutes.

Nutrients per serving (1 appetizer): Calories: 68, Total Fat: 3 g, Cholesterol: 22 mg, Sodium: 78 mg, Protein: 3 g, Dietary Fiber: trace

*Favorite recipe from **Colorado Potato Administrative Committee***

Herbed Potato Chips ▶

Nonstick olive oil cooking
   spray
2 medium unpeeled red skinned
   potatoes
1 tablespoon olive oil
2 tablespoons minced fresh dill,
   thyme or rosemary *or*
    2 teaspoons dried dill weed,
   thyme or rosemary

¼ teaspoon garlic salt
⅛ teaspoon black pepper
1¼ cups nonfat sour cream

1. Preheat oven to 450°F. Spray large nonstick baking sheets with nonstick cooking spray; set aside.

2. Cut potatoes crosswise into very thin slices, about ¹⁄₁₆ inch thick. Pat dry with paper towels. Arrange potato slices in single layer on prepared baking sheets; coat potatoes with nonstick cooking spray.

3. Bake 10 minutes; turn slices over. Brush with oil. Combine dill, garlic salt and pepper in small bowl; sprinkle evenly onto potato slices. Continue baking 5 to 10 minutes or until potatoes are golden brown. Cool on baking sheets. Serve with sour cream.

Makes about 60 chips

***Nutrients per serving** (10 chips, about 3 tablespoons sour cream): Calories: 76 , Total Fat: 2 g, Saturated Fat: trace, Cholesterol: 0 mg, Sodium: 113 mg, Protein: 6 g, Dietary Fiber: trace*

Potato Pancake Appetizers

3 medium Colorado russet
    potatoes peeled and grated
1 egg
2 tablespoons all-purpose flour
1 teaspoon salt
¼ teaspoon black pepper
1 cup grated carrot (1 large)

1½ cups grated zucchini (2 small)
½ cup low-fat sour cream or
    plain yogurt
2 tablespoons finely chopped
    fresh basil
1 tablespoon chopped chives *or*
    1½ teaspoons chili powder

Preheat oven to 425°F. Wrap potatoes in several layers of paper towels; squeeze to remove excess moisture. Beat egg, flour, salt and pepper in large bowl. Add potatoes, carrot and zucchini; mix well. Oil 2 nonstick baking sheets. Place vegetable mixture by heaping spoonfuls onto baking sheets; flatten slightly. Bake 8 to 15 minutes until bottoms are browned. Turn; bake 5 to 10 minutes more. Stir together sour cream and herbs; serve with warm pancakes.
Makes about 24 appetizer pancakes

Nutrients per serving *(1 pancake): Calories: 29, Total Fat: 1 g, Cholesterol: 11 mg, Sodium: 96 mg, Protein: 1 g, Dietary Fiber: 1 g*

Favorite recipe from **Colorado Potato Administrative Committee**

Cheesy Potato Skins

2 tablespoons grated Parmesan
    cheese
3 cloves garlic, finely chopped
2 teaspoons dried rosemary
½ teaspoon salt

¼ teaspoon black pepper
4 baking potatoes, baked
2 egg whites, slightly beaten
½ cup (2 ounces) shredded part-
    skim mozzarella cheese

Preheat oven to 400°F. Combine Parmesan cheese, garlic, rosemary, salt and pepper in small bowl. Cut potatoes lengthwise in half. Remove pulp, leaving ¼-inch-thick shells. Reserve pulp for another use. Cut potatoes lengthwise into wedges. Place on baking sheet. Brush with egg whites; sprinkle with Parmesan cheese mixture. Bake 20 minutes. Sprinkle with mozzarella cheese; bake until mozzarella cheese is melted. Serve with salsa, if desired.
Makes 8 servings

Nutrients per serving: *Calories: 90, Total Fat: 2 g, Saturated Fat: 1 g, Cholesterol: 5 mg, Sodium: 215 mg, Protein: 5 g, Dietary Fiber: 2 g*

Hot & Spicy Ribbon Chips ▲

6 medium unpeeled Colorado
    russet potatoes
1 tablespoon plus 1 teaspoon
    salt, divided
Vegetable oil

1 tablespoon chili powder
1 teaspoon garlic salt
¼ to ½ teaspoon ground red
    pepper

With vegetable peeler, make thin lengthwise potato ribbons. Place in large bowl with 1-quart ice water mixed with 1 tablespoon salt. Heat oil in deep-fat fryer or heavy pan to 365°F. Combine chili powder, remaining 1 teaspoon salt, garlic salt and red pepper; set aside. Drain potatoes and pat dry with paper towels. Fry potatoes in batches until crisp and golden brown; remove with slotted spoon to paper towels. Sprinkle with chili powder mixture.   *Makes 8 to 12 servings*

Nutrients per serving *(⅛ of recipe): Calories: 91, Total Fat: 4 g, Cholesterol: 0 mg, Sodium: 343 mg, Protein: 2 g, Dietary Fiber: 1 g*

*Favorite recipe from **Colorado Potato Administrative Committee***

COMFORTING
Soups & Stews

You'll find everything from ever-popular Cheesy Potato Soup to trendy Spicy African Chick-Pea and Sweet Potato Stew in this splendid collection.

Potato & Cheddar Soup ▶

2 cups red-skinned potatoes, peeled and cut into cubes
3 tablespoons margarine or butter
1 small onion, finely chopped
3 tablespoons all-purpose flour
Ground red pepper

Black pepper
3 cups milk
½ teaspoon salt
1 cup cubed cooked ham
1 cup (4 ounces) shredded Cheddar cheese

Bring 2 cups water to a boil in large saucepan. Add potatoes; simmer until tender. Drain, reserving liquid. Measure 1 cup reserved liquid, adding water if necessary. Melt margarine in same saucepan over medium heat. Add onion; cook and stir until tender but not brown. Stir in flour; season to taste with red and black pepper. Cook 3 to 4 minutes. Gradually add potatoes, reserved liquid, milk and salt to onion mixture; stir well. Add ham. Simmer over low heat 5 minutes, stirring frequently. Remove from heat; cool 5 minutes. Stir in cheese until melted. *Makes 3 to 4 servings*

Chunky Garden Stew ▶

Spicy Hot Sauce (recipe
follows)
1 tablespoon olive or canola oil
3 medium Colorado Sangre red
potatoes, cut into chunks
1 large carrot, sliced diagonally
1 medium onion, quartered
1 large yellow squash or
zucchini, sliced
1 Japanese eggplant *or* ½ regular
eggplant, cut into cubes
2 celery stalks, sliced
1 small red or green bell pepper,
cut into chunks

1 teaspoon ground cinnamon
1 teaspoon coriander
1 teaspoon turmeric
½ teaspoon ground cumin
½ teaspoon ground cardamom
½ teaspoon salt
2 cans (14½ ounces each)
vegetable broth *or* 1½ cups
water
1 can (15 ounces) chick-peas,
drained
⅔ cup raisins
6 cups hot cooked rice

Prepare Spicy Hot Sauce; set aside. Heat oil in Dutch oven over medium-high heat. Add potatoes and carrot; cook and stir 5 minutes. Add onion, squash, eggplant, celery, bell pepper, spices and salt; cook and stir 3 to 5 minutes. Add broth, chick-peas and raisins; bring to a simmer. Simmer, covered, about 15 minutes or until potatoes are tender. Serve vegetable stew over rice. Serve with Spicy Hot Sauce.   *Makes 5 to 6 servings*

Spicy Hot Sauce

⅓ cup coarsely chopped cilantro
¼ cup water
1 tablespoon olive or canola oil
2 cloves garlic
½ teaspoon salt
½ teaspoon turmeric

¼ to ½ teaspoon ground red
pepper
¼ teaspoon sugar
¼ teaspoon ground cumin
¼ teaspoon ground cardamom
¼ teaspoon ground coriander

Combine all ingredients in blender; process until smooth. Adjust flavors to taste.

Makes about ½ cup sauce

Nutrients per serving (¹/₅ *of recipe*): *Calories: 456 g, Total Fat: 7 g, Cholesterol: 0 mg, Sodium: 397 mg, Protein: 15 g, Dietary Fiber: 12 g*

Favorite recipe from **Colorado Potato Administrative Committee**

Sweet Potato and Ham Soup ▶

1 tablespoon margarine or
   butter
1 small leek, sliced
1 clove garlic, minced
½ pound ham, cut into ½-inch
   cubes
2 medium sweet potatoes, peeled
   and cut into ¾-inch cubes

4 cups canned chicken broth
½ teaspoon dried thyme leaves,
   crushed
2 ounces fresh spinach, coarsely
   chopped

1. Melt margarine in large saucepan over medium heat. Add leek and garlic. Cook and stir until leek is limp.

2. Add ham, sweet potatoes, broth and thyme to saucepan. Bring to a boil over high heat. Reduce heat to medium-low. Cook 10 minutes or until sweet potatoes are tender.

3. Stir spinach into soup. Simmer, uncovered, 2 minutes or until spinach is wilted. Serve immediately.

Makes 6 servings

Farmer's Cold Tater Soup

2 to 3 Colorado potatoes, peeled
2 large onions, minced
2 leeks, minced (white parts
   only)
4 cups water

1 cup canned chicken broth
1 tablespoon butter, melted
1 tablespoon flour
2 cups hot milk*
   Chopped chives for garnish

Combine potatoes, onions, leeks and water in large saucepan over high heat. Bring to a boil. Reduce heat to medium-low. Simmer 25 minutes or until potatoes are tender. Process vegetables in blender or food processor until smooth; return to saucepan. Add broth. Combine butter and flour until blended. Stir into potato mixture. Bring to a boil. Boil 1 minute. Stir in hot milk. Cool soup to room temperature; refrigerate until cold. Garnish with chopped chives.

Makes 4 to 6 servings

*For a richer soup, replace 1 cup milk with 1 cup half-and-half.

Nutrients per serving *(¼ of recipe): Calories: 216, Total Fat: 6 g, Cholesterol: 17 mg, Sodium: 348 mg, Protein: 8 g, Dietary Fiber: 3 g*

*Favorite recipe from **Colorado Potato Administrative Committee***

New England Clam Chowder ▶

24 medium clams
  Salt
1 bottle (8 ounces) clam juice
3 medium potatoes, cut into
  ½-inch-thick slices
¼ teaspoon dried thyme leaves,
  crushed
¼ teaspoon ground white pepper

4 slices bacon, cut crosswise into
  ¼-inch-wide strips
1 medium onion, chopped
⅓ cup all-purpose flour
2 cups milk
1 cup half-and-half
  Oyster crackers
  Fresh thyme for garnish

1. Scrub clams. Soak clams in mixture of ⅓ cup salt to 1 gallon water 20 minutes. Drain water; repeat. Place clams on tray and refrigerate 1 hour to help clams relax. Shuck clams; place clams and their juice in strainer over bowl. Strain clam juice through triple thickness of dampened cheesecloth into 2-cup measure. Coarsely chop clams; set aside.

2. Add bottled clam juice and enough water to clam juice in glass measure to total 2 cups; place clam juice mixture in Dutch oven. Add potatoes, thyme and pepper. Bring to a boil. Reduce heat to low. Simmer 15 minutes or until potatoes are tender, stirring occasionally.

3. Meanwhile, cook bacon in medium skillet over medium heat until almost crisp. Add onion; cook until tender but not brown.

4. Stir flour into bacon mixture. Whisk in milk using wire whisk. Cook until mixture boils and thickens. Add bacon mixture and half-and-half to potato mixture. Add clams; heat until clams are firm. Serve chowder with oyster crackers. Garnish, if desired.

Makes 6 main-dish servings

Spicy African Chick-Pea and Sweet Potato Stew

Spice Paste (recipe follows)
1½ pounds sweet potatoes, peeled and cubed
2 cups canned vegetable broth or water
1 can (16 ounces) chick-peas, drained and rinsed
1 can (14½ ounces) plum tomatoes, undrained and chopped

1½ cups sliced fresh okra *or*
1 package (10 ounces) frozen cut okra, thawed
Yellow Couscous (recipe follows)
Hot pepper sauce
Fresh cilantro for garnish

1. Prepare Spice Paste.

2. Combine sweet potatoes, broth, chick-peas, tomatoes and juice, okra and Spice Paste in large saucepan. Bring to a boil over high heat. Reduce heat to low. Cover and simmer 15 minutes. Uncover; simmer 10 minutes or until vegetables are tender.

3. Meanwhile, prepare Yellow Couscous.

4. Serve stew with couscous and pepper sauce. Garnish, if desired.

Makes 4 servings

Spice Paste

6 cloves garlic, peeled
1 teaspoon coarse salt
2 teaspoons sweet paprika
1½ teaspoons cumin seeds

1 teaspoon cracked black pepper
½ teaspoon ground ginger
½ teaspoon ground allspice
1 tablespoon olive oil

Process garlic and salt in blender or small food processor until garlic is finely chopped. Add remaining spices. Process 15 seconds. While blender is running, pour oil through cover opening; process until mixture forms paste.

Yellow Couscous

1 tablespoon olive oil
5 green onions, sliced
1⅔ cups water
⅛ teaspoon saffron threads *or*
    ½ teaspoon ground turmeric

¼ teaspoon salt
1 cup precooked couscous*

1. Heat oil in medium saucepan over medium heat until hot. Add onions; cook and stir 4 minutes. Add water, saffron and salt. Bring to a boil. Stir in couscous. Remove from heat. Cover; let stand 5 minutes.   *Makes 3 cups*

*Check ingredient label for "precooked semolina."

Cheesy Potato Soup

4 baking potatoes, scrubbed
    (about 1½ pounds)
2 tablespoons butter
1 medium onion, sliced
2 tablespoons all-purpose flour
1 teaspoon beef bouillon
    granules
2 cups water

1 can (12 ounces) evaporated
    milk
1 cup (4 ounces) shredded
    Wisconsin brick cheese
1 teaspoon chopped parsley
¾ teaspoon Worcestershire sauce
¾ teaspoon salt
¾ teaspoon black pepper

Microwave Directions: Pierce potatoes several times with fork. Microwave on paper towel at HIGH 10 to 12 minutes or until potatoes are soft; cool. Place butter and onion in large bowl. Microwave at HIGH 2 minutes or until tender. Stir in flour. Stir in bouillon granules and water until well blended. Microwave at HIGH 2 minutes or until onion mixture is heated. Scoop out potato pulp, leaving it in chunks. Add potato pulp, evaporated milk, cheese, parsley, Worcestershire, salt and pepper to onion mixture. Microwave at HIGH 2½ to 4 minutes or until cheese is melted and soup is hot.
          Makes 6 servings

Nutrients per serving: Calories: 308, Total Fat: 14 g, Cholesterol: 45 mg, Sodium: 614 mg, Protein: 12 g

*Favorite recipe from **Wisconsin Milk Marketing Board***

POTATO
Salads Galore

Potato salads aren't just for picnics–they're a hit any time of the year. Dress them up with a touch of pesto, crisp change-of-pace snow peas or sweet Italian sausages and wait for the applause.

Potato & Prosciutto Salad ▶

3 medium Colorado Sangre red
    potatoes, unpeeled
½ pound green beans, trimmed
    and cut into 2½-inch pieces
1 red bell pepper, thinly sliced
1½ cups frozen corn, thawed
6 ounces mozzarella cheese, cut
    into ½-inch cubes
3 ounces thinly sliced prosciutto
    or ham, cut into strips

3 green onions, sliced
⅓ cup olive oil
¼ cup lemon juice
2 tablespoons water
1 to 2 cloves garlic, minced
1 tablespoon chopped fresh
    thyme *or* 1½ teaspoon dried
    thyme leaves
Salt and black pepper

Cook potatoes in boiling water 25 minutes until tender. Drain; cool. Cut into ½-inch-thick slices; cut into quarters. Cook green beans in boiling water until tender. Drain; cool. Combine potatoes, beans, bell pepper, corn, cheese, prosciutto and onions in large bowl. Whisk together oil, lemon juice, water, garlic and thyme. Pour dressing over potato mixture; toss to coat. Season to taste. *Makes 6 to 8 servings*

Nutrients per Serving (¹⁄₆ *of recipe*): *Calories: 237, Total Fat: 12 g, Cholesterol: 17 mg, Sodium: 254 mg, Protein: 11 g, Dietary Fiber: 3 g*

Favorite recipe from **Colorado Potato Administrative Committee**

Salad Niçoise

1 box (9 ounces) BIRDS EYE® frozen Cut Green Beans

1 head Boston or green leaf lettuce

1 can (16 ounces) whole potatoes, drained and cut into ¼-inch slices

1 can (6 ounces) tuna packed in water, drained

2 tomatoes, cut into wedges

⅓ cup Greek or black olives

⅓ cup Caesar salad dressing

COOK green beans according to package directions. Drain and rinse under cold water to cool; drain well.

ARRANGE lettuce leaves on serving platter. Arrange beans, potatoes, tuna, tomatoes and olives in separate piles on lettuce.

DRIZZLE dressing over salad.   *Makes about 4 servings*

Prep Time: 10 minutes   **Cook Time:** 5 minutes

Pear and Potato Salad

1 cup BLUE DIAMOND® Blanched Slivered Almonds

1 tablespoon olive oil

½ cup mayonnaise

2 cloves garlic, finely chopped

½ teaspoon salt

¼ teaspoon grated fresh ginger *or* ⅛ teaspoon ground ginger

¼ teaspoon black pepper

½ cup chopped fresh parsley

½ pound new potatoes, peeled and diced

1 pound slightly firm pears, peeled, cored, diced and tossed with 1 tablespoon lemon juice

1 medium red bell pepper, diced

½ cup thinly sliced green onions (including white and green parts)

Sauté almonds in oil until golden; set aside. Combine mayonnaise, garlic, salt, ginger and black pepper in medium bowl. Fold in parsley; set aside. Cook potatoes in salted, boiling water until just tender. (Do not overcook.) Drain; while still warm, combine with dressing. Cool to room temperature. Fold in pears, bell pepper and green onions. Chill. Just before serving, fold in almonds.   *Makes 4 to 6 servings*

Santa Fe Potato Salad ▼

5 medium white potatoes
½ cup vegetable oil
¼ cup red wine vinegar
1 package (1.0 ounce) LAWRYS® Taco Spices & Seasonings
1 can (7 ounces) whole kernel corn, drained
⅔ cup sliced celery
⅔ cup shredded carrot
⅔ cup chopped red or green bell pepper
2 cans (2.25 ounces each) sliced ripe olives, drained
½ cup chopped red onion
2 tomatoes, wedged and halved

In large saucepan, cook potatoes in boiling water until tender, about 30 minutes; drain. Let cool slightly; cube. In small bowl, combine oil, vinegar and Taco Spices & Seasonings; blend well. Add to warm potatoes; toss gently to coat. Cover; refrigerate at least 1 hour. Gently fold in remaining ingredients. Chill thoroughly.

Makes 8 servings

Presentation: Serve chilled with deli sandwiches or hamburgers.

Creamier Version: Prepare potatoes as above. Replace the vinegar and oil with ½ cup *each* mayonnaise, dairy sour cream and salsa. Mix with Taco Spices & Seasonings and continue as directed above.

Potato-Bean Salad Vinaigrette ▶

1½ pounds unpeeled red-skinned
    potatoes, scrubbed and
    cubed
1½ teaspoons salt, divided
¼ cup olive oil
2 tablespoons red wine vinegar
1 clove garlic, minced
1 tablespoon minced fresh
    oregano *or* 1 teaspoon dried
    oregano leaves, crushed

¼ teaspoon black pepper
1 can (15 ounces) Great
    Northern beans, rinsed and
    drained
1 cup finely chopped celery
1 cup finely chopped red bell
    pepper
½ cup sliced ripe olives
    (optional)
¼ cup finely chopped red onion

1. Place potatoes in medium saucepan; add water to cover and 1 teaspoon salt. Bring to a boil over medium-high heat. Reduce heat to medium-low. Simmer; uncovered, 5 to 7 minutes until potatoes are tender when pierced with fork. (Do not overcook.) Drain.

2. Whisk together oil, vinegar, garlic, oregano, remaining ½ teaspoon salt and black pepper in large bowl until mixture thickens.

3. Add beans, celery, bell pepper, olives, if desired, and onion. Toss gently. Add warm potatoes; toss gently until vegetables are coated. Let salad stand at least 10 minutes to marinate. Serve warm or at room temperature.   *Makes 4 to 6 servings*

Tomato Potato Salad

1½ pounds fresh California
    tomatoes, seeded and cubed
½ cup chopped red onion
¼ cup chopped fresh cilantro
1½ teaspoons ground cumin

1 teaspoon chopped fresh garlic
¼ teaspoon black pepper
1½ pounds red potatoes, cooked
    and cubed
½ cup plain nonfat yogurt

Combine tomatoes, onion and seasonings in large bowl. Add potatoes and yogurt; gently toss to coat.   *Makes 6 to 8 servings*

*Favorite recipe from **California Tomato Board***

Grilled Steak & Potato Salad ▼

Marinade

- ¼ cup warm water
- 3 tablespoons herb-flavored oil*
- 2 tablespoons balsamic vinegar
- 2 tablespoons seasoned rice vinegar
- 1 teaspoon grainy Dijon mustard
- ¼ teaspoon salt

Salad

- 1 pound lean boneless top sirloin steak
- 4 medium Colorado Sangre red potatoes, scrubbed
- 2 small ears corn, quartered *or* 1 large ear, cut into eighths
- 1 small red bell pepper, cut into rings or strips
- 1 large zucchini, sliced
- 8 medium mushrooms, halved
- ½ red onion, sliced
  Salt and black pepper
  Salad greens

To prepare marinade, whisk together marinade ingredients in bowl. Place steak in large resealable plastic food storage bag. Add about 2 tablespoons marinade. Seal bag. Marinate in refrigerator 1 hour or longer.

Meanwhile, steam or microwave potatoes until tender; cool. Cut potatoes into thick slices or chunks; arrange potatoes, corn, bell pepper, zucchini, mushrooms and onion in rows in glass 13×9-inch baking dish. Add remaining marinade. Marinate 30 minutes or longer. Remove vegetables from marinade, reserving marinade. Grill vegetables over hot coals until tender. Season to taste with salt. Remove steak from marinade, discarding any remaining marinade. Season to taste with salt and pepper. Grill over hot coals to desired doneness. Place salad greens on each of four serving plates. Arrange vegetables on greens. Slice steak on the diagonal and arrange on plates. Pour reserved marinade over salad. *Makes 4 servings*

*Olive oil combined with your choice of chopped fresh herbs or dried herb leaves can be substituted for herb-flavored oil.

Nutrients per serving: *Calories: 452, Total Fat: 16 g, Cholesterol: 77 mg, Sodium: 345 mg, Protein: 33 g, Dietary Fiber: 6 g*

Favorite recipe from **Colorado Potato Administrative Committee**

Gloria's Pesto Potato Salad

Dressing
  1 cup mayonnaise
  2 tablespoons prepared pesto

Salad
  4 cups diced peeled cooked
    potatoes
  ½ cup chopped celery

½ cup sliced green onions
½ cup diced red bell pepper
1½ cups (6 ounces) cubed
    Wisconsin Monterey Jack
    cheese
  1 tablespoon grated Wisconsin
    Parmesan cheese

Combine dressing ingredients in small bowl. Combine potatoes, celery, onions, pepper and Monterey Jack cheese in medium bowl. Add dressing; toss lightly. Sprinkle with Parmesan cheese. Chill. *Makes 6 servings*

Tip: Wisconsin Havarti cheese delivers the same creamy texture as Monterey Jack cheese and can be substituted for it in this recipe.

Favorite recipe from **Wisconsin Milk Marketing Board**

Potato Salad with Sweet Sausages and Mushrooms

3 pounds (16 to 20) small red potatoes, scrubbed and quartered
2 pounds sweet Italian sausages
½ cup dry red wine
⅔ cup plus 2 tablespoons extra-virgin olive oil, divided
1 pound mushrooms, sliced
1 teaspoon lemon juice
3 teaspoons TABASCO® brand Pepper Sauce, divided
¾ cup chopped green onions
⅓ cup dry white wine
⅓ cup chicken broth or stock
2 tablespoons Dijon mustard
½ teaspoon salt
¼ teaspoon black pepper

Cook potatoes in boiling water in large saucepan 15 to 20 minutes or until fork tender. Drain and cool. Cut into ¼-inch-thick slices. Place in large bowl.

Meanwhile, preheat oven to 350°F. Place sausages in single layer in baking dish; pierce several times with fork. Bake 15 minutes. Turn and bake 15 minutes longer. Add red wine; turn sausages. Bake 8 minutes. Turn sausages once more; bake 7 minutes longer or until cooked through. Remove sausages; cool. Cut into 1-inch-thick slices. Add to potatoes.

Heat 2 tablespoons olive oil in large skillet over medium-high heat. Add mushrooms; cook and stir 5 minutes or until most of liquid evaporates. Sprinkle with lemon juice and 1½ teaspoon TABASCO® Sauce. Add to potato mixture with green onions; toss lightly to mix.

Combine white wine, broth, mustard, salt, pepper and remaining 1½ teaspoons TABASCO® Sauce in food processor or blender. Process until well blended. While food processor is running, slowly add remaining ⅔ cup olive oil; process until blended. Pour mixture over salad; toss to coat. Serve warm or at room temperature; or cover and refrigerate overnight.

Makes 12 servings

SPAM™ Skillet Potato Salad

1 (12-ounce) can SPAM®
   Luncheon Meat, cut into
   strips
½ cup chopped green onions
½ cup chopped green bell pepper
3 medium potatoes, boiled and
   diced

1½ cups (6 ounces) shredded
   sharp Cheddar cheese
¼ cup mayonnaise or salad
   dressing

In large skillet over medium heat, sauté SPAM,® green onions and bell pepper until SPAM® is lightly browned. Add potatoes, cheese and mayonnaise. Heat just until cheese begins to melt.

Makes 6 servings

Nutrients per serving: *Calories: 353, Total Fat: 25 g, Cholesterol: 80 mg, Sodium: 792 mg, Protein: 18 g*

Wisconsin True Blue Potato Salad

1¼ cups dairy sour cream
2 tablespoons minced parsley
2 tablespoons tarragon-flavored
   white wine vinegar
½ teaspoon salt
½ teaspoon celery seed
⅛ teaspoon black pepper

¾ cup (3-ounces) crumbled
   Wisconsin Blue cheese
4 cups cubed cooked potatoes
½ cup sliced water chestnuts
½ cup diced celery
½ cup green onion slices

Combine sour cream, parsley, vinegar and seasonings in medium bowl; mix well. Stir in cheese. Combine potatoes, water chestnuts, celery and onions in large bowl. Add sour cream mixture; toss lightly. Chill.

Makes 6 servings

Nutrients per serving: *Calories: 240, Total Fat: 14 g, Cholesterol: 32 mg, Sodium: 416 mg, Protein: 6 g*

Favorite recipe from **Wisconsin Milk Marketing Board**

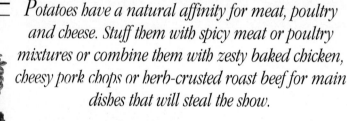

POTATOES
Take Center Stage

Potatoes have a natural affinity for meat, poultry and cheese. Stuff them with spicy meat or poultry mixtures or combine them with zesty baked chicken, cheesy pork chops or herb-crusted roast beef for main dishes that will steal the show.

Baked Potatoes with Tuna and Broccoli in Cheese Sauce ▶

2 medium baking potatoes (6 to 8 ounces each)
1 package (10 ounces) frozen broccoli in cheese sauce
1 can (6 ounces) STARKIST® Solid White Tuna, drained and chunked

1 teaspoon chili powder
¼ cup minced green onions, including tops
2 slices cooked, crumbled bacon

Microwave Directions: Wash and pierce potatoes; microwave on HIGH 8 minutes. Remove from microwave. Wrap in foil; let stand to finish cooking while preparing broccoli. Microwave vented pouch of broccoli on HIGH 5 minutes. In medium microwavable bowl, combine tuna and chili powder. Gently stir in broccoli. Cover; heat on HIGH 1½ more minutes or until heated through. Cut potatoes in half lengthwise. Top with broccoli-tuna mixture; sprinkle with onions and bacon. *Makes 2 servings*

Prep Time: 20 minutes

Note: Recipe can easily be doubled for 4—just cook a little longer in the microwave.

Potato Straw Cake with Ham & Gruyère ▶

4 medium Colorado russet
variety potatoes
1 tablespoon water
2 teaspoons lemon juice
2 teaspoons Dijon mustard
1 cup (4 ounces) thinly sliced
ham, cut into strips
¾ cup (3 ounces) shredded
Gruyère cheese

½ teaspoon dried tarragon,
crushed *or* ¼ teaspoon
ground nutmeg
3 to 4 green onions, thinly
sliced, white parts separated
from dark green tops
3 teaspoons oil, divided
Salt and black pepper

Peel and grate potatoes. Place in bowl with water to cover; let stand at room temperature about ½ hour while preparing other ingredients. Blend 1 tablespoon water, lemon juice and mustard in bowl. Stir in ham, cheese, tarragon and white parts of onions. Reserve green onion tops. Drain potatoes, wrap in several thicknesses of paper towels or clean dish towel and squeeze to wring out much of liquid.

Heat 1½ teaspoons oil in heavy 8- or 10-inch nonstick skillet over high heat. Add half the potatoes, pressing into skillet with back of spoon. Season to taste with salt and pepper. Spread evenly with ham mixture. Cover with remaining potatoes. Season to taste with salt and pepper. Reduce heat to medium-low. Cover and cook 20 to 30 minutes or until potatoes are crisp and golden brown on bottom. Uncover and place rimless baking sheet over skillet. Invert skillet onto baking sheet to release potato cake. Add remaining 1½ teaspoons oil to skillet. Slide cake into skillet, uncooked side down. Cook, uncovered, over medium-low heat 10 to 15 minutes. Increase heat to medium-high and cook until brown and crisp, shaking pan several times to prevent sticking. Slide potato cake onto serving plate. Garnish with reserved green onion tops. Cut into wedges.

Makes 5 to 6 servings

Nutrients per serving (*¹/₅ of recipe): Calories: 204, Total Fat: 8 g, Cholesterol: 26 mg, Sodium: 305 mg, Protein: 11 g, Dietary Fiber: 2 g*

*Favorite recipe from **Colorado Potato Administrative Committee***

Tex-Mex Ground Turkey Potato Boats ▲

2 medium potatoes
½ pound ground turkey
½ cup onion, chopped
1 clove garlic, minced
1 can (8 ounces) stewed
    tomatoes
1 teaspoon chili powder

¼ teaspoon salt
¼ teaspoon dried oregano leaves,
    crushed
¼ teaspoon ground cumin
¼ teaspoon red pepper flakes
½ cup (2 ounces) shredded
    reduced-fat Cheddar cheese

1. Preheat oven to 400°F. Pierce potatoes several times with fork. Bake 50 to 60 minutes or until soft. Cool slightly. *Reduce oven temperature to 375°F.*

2. Slice potatoes in half, lengthwise. Scoop out pulp with spoon, leaving ¼-inch shell. (Reserve potato pulp for other use.) Place potato shells on jelly-roll pan or baking sheet.

3. Place turkey, onion and garlic in medium skillet. Cook over medium-high heat 5 minutes or until turkey is no longer pink; drain. Add tomatoes, chili powder, salt, oregano, cumin and red pepper flakes to turkey in skillet. Cook 15 minutes or until most of liquid has evaporated.

4. Spoon turkey mixture evenly into potato shells; sprinkle with cheese. Bake 15 minutes or until cheese melts. *Makes 4 servings*

Nutrients per serving: Calories: 209, Total Fat: 7 g, Cholesterol: 51 mg, Sodium: 446 mg, Protein: 16 g

Favorite recipe from **National Turkey Federation**

Herb-Crusted Roast Beef and Potatoes

1 (4½-pound) eye of round or sirloin tip beef roast
¾ cup plus 2 tablespoons FILIPPO BERIO® Olive Oil, divided
Salt and freshly ground black pepper
2 tablespoons paprika

2 pounds small red-skin potatoes, cut in half
1 cup dry bread crumbs
1 teaspoon dried thyme leaves
1 teaspoon dried rosemary
½ teaspoon salt
¼ teaspoon freshly ground black pepper

Preheat oven to 325°F. Brush roast with 2 tablespoons olive oil. Season to taste with salt and pepper. Place in large roasting pan; insert meat thermometer into center of thickest part of roast. Roast 45 minutes.

Meanwhile, in large bowl, combine ½ cup olive oil and paprika. Add potatoes; toss until lightly coated. In small bowl, combine bread crumbs, thyme, rosemary, ½ teaspoon salt, ¼ teaspoon pepper and remaining ¼ cup olive oil.

Carefully remove roast from oven. Place potatoes around roast. Press bread crumb mixture onto top of roast to form crust. Sprinkle any remaining bread crumb mixture over potatoes. Roast an additional 40 to 45 minutes or until meat thermometer registers 145°F for medium-rare or until desired doneness is reached. Transfer roast to carving board; tent with foil. Let stand 5 to 10 minutes before carving. Cut into ¼-inch-thick slices. Serve immediately with potatoes, spooning any bread crumb mixture from roasting pan onto meat. *Makes 8 servings*

Country Kielbasa Kabobs ▶

½ cup **GREY POUPON® COUNTRY DIJON® Mustard**
½ cup apricot preserves
⅓ cup minced green onions
1 pound kielbasa, cut into 1-inch pieces
1 large apple, cored and cut into wedges

½ cup frozen pearl onions, thawed
6 small red skin potatoes, parboiled and cut into halves
3 cups shredded red and green cabbage, steamed

Soak 6 (10-inch) wooden skewers in water for 30 minutes. In small bowl, blend mustard, preserves and green onions; set aside ¼ cup mixture.

Alternately thread kielbasa, apple, pearl onions and potatoes on skewers. Grill or broil kabobs for 12 to 15 minutes or until done, turning and brushing with remaining mustard mixture. Heat reserved mustard mixture and toss with steamed cabbage. Serve heated through with kabobs. Garnish as desired.   *Makes 6 servings*

Easy Chicken and Potato Dinner

1 package (2 pounds) bone-in chicken breasts or thighs
1 pound potatoes, cut into wedges
½ cup **KRAFT® Zesty Italian Dressing**

1 tablespoon Italian seasoning
½ cup **KRAFT® 100% Grated Parmesan Cheese**

PLACE chicken and potatoes in 13×9-inch baking pan.

POUR dressing over chicken and potatoes. Sprinkle evenly with Italian seasoning and cheese.

BAKE at 400°F for 1 hour or until chicken is cooked through.   *Makes 4 servings*

Pork with Couscous & Root Vegetables ▶

1 teaspoon vegetable oil
½ pound pork tenderloin, thinly
    sliced
2 sweet potatoes, peeled and cut
    into chunks
2 medium turnips, peeled and
    cut into chunks
1 carrot, sliced
3 cloves garlic, finely chopped
1 can (about 15 ounces) chick-
    peas rinsed and drained

1 cup reduced-sodium vegetable
    broth
½ cup pitted prunes, cut into
    thirds
1 teaspoon ground cumin
½ teaspoon ground cinnamon
¼ teaspoon ground allspice
¼ teaspoon ground nutmeg
¼ teaspoon black pepper
1 cup cooked couscous
2 tablespoons dried currants

1. Heat oil in large nonstick skillet over medium-high heat until hot. Add pork, sweet potatoes, turnips, carrot and garlic. Cook and stir 5 minutes. Stir in chick-peas, broth, prunes, cumin, cinnamon, allspice, nutmeg and pepper. Cover; bring to a boil over high heat. Reduce heat to medium-low. Simmer 30 minutes until vegetables are tender.

2. Serve pork and vegetables on couscous. Top servings evenly with currants. Garnish with fresh thyme, if desired.
                    Makes 4 servings

Nutrients per serving: *Calories: 508, Total Fat: 6 g, Saturated Fat: 1 g, Cholesterol: 30 mg, Sodium: 500 mg, Protein: 26 g, Dietary Fiber: 17 g*

Potato & Lamb Cobbler

1¼ pounds boneless American lamb (leg or shoulder), cut into ¾-inch pieces

¼ cup all-purpose flour

2 teaspoons olive oil

2 cups lamb stock *or* 1 can (14½ ounces) beef broth plus ¼ cup water, divided

¾ pound mushrooms (wild or cultivated), sliced

1 onion, chopped

2 garlic cloves, minced

1 pound red-skinned potatoes, cut into ¾-inch cubes

1½ teaspoons chopped fresh thyme *or* 1 teaspoon dried thyme leaves, crushed

1½ teaspoons chopped fresh rosemary *or* 1 teaspoon dried rosemary, crushed

3 tablespoons finely chopped fresh parsley

Cobbler Dough (recipe follows)

1 egg yolk

1 tablespoon milk

Season lamb to taste with salt and pepper; coat with flour. Heat oil in Dutch oven over medium-high heat. Add lamb and brown on all sides. Remove lamb from pan and reserve. Add ½ cup stock, mushrooms, onion and garlic; cook until liquid has evaporated and onion is tender, stirring to scrape all brown bits from pan. Add remaining 1½ cups stock, potatoes, thyme and rosemary; cover and bring to a boil. Reduce heat to low; add lamb. Simmer, partially covered, 45 minutes or until lamb is tender. Season to taste with additional salt and pepper, if desired. Stir in chopped parsley.*

Preheat oven to 375°F. Prepare Cobbler Dough. On a lightly floured surface, roll dough to about ¼-inch thickness. Using a cookie cutter, cut dough into leaves or other shapes; reroll scraps and cut more shapes. Ladle lamb mixture into 1½-quart casserole or 10-inch deep-dish pie plate. Top with dough cutouts, clustering and overlapping leaves slightly, allowing open spaces for steam to escape. Beat together egg yolk and milk; brush dough with mixture. Bake about 15 to 20 minutes or until top is golden brown.

Makes 6 servings

*Sauce should be the consistency of gravy. If it's too thin, remove lamb and vegetables to casserole with a slotted spoon. Boil the sauce to reduce it to desired consistency.

Cobbler Dough: Combine 1 cup flour, 1 tablespoon sugar, 1 teaspoon baking powder and ½ teaspoon salt in a small bowl. Stir in ½ cup heavy cream; mix just until blended. Gather dough into ball.

*Favorite recipe from **American Lamb Council***

Cheesy Pork Chops 'n' Potatoes

1 jar (8 ounces) pasteurized
    processed cheese spread
1 tablespoon vegetable oil
6 thin pork chops, ¼ to ½ inch
    thick
    Seasoned salt
½ cup milk

4 cups frozen cottage fries
1⅓ cups (2.8 ounce can)
    FRENCH'S® French Fried
    Onions
1 package (10 ounces) frozen
    broccoli spears,* thawed and
    drained

Preheat oven to 350°F. Spoon cheese spread into 8×12-inch baking dish; place in oven just until cheese melts, about 5 minutes. Meanwhile, in large skillet, heat oil. Brown pork chops on both sides; drain. Sprinkle chops with seasoned salt; set aside. Using fork, stir milk into melted cheese until well blended. Stir cottage fries and ⅔ *cup* French Fried Onions into cheese mixture. Divide broccoli spears into 6 small bunches. Arrange bunches of spears over potato mixture with flowerets around edges of dish. Arrange chops over broccoli *stalks*. Bake, covered, at 350°F for 35 to 40 minutes or until pork chops are no longer pink. Top chops with remaining ⅔ *cup* onions; bake, uncovered, 5 minutes or until onions are golden brown. *Makes 4 to 6 servings*

*1 small head fresh broccoli (about ½ pound) may be substituted for frozen spears. Divide into spears and cook 3 to 4 minutes before using.

Microwave Directions: Omit oil. Reduce milk to ¼ cup. In 8×12-inch microwave-safe dish, place cheese spread and milk. Cook, covered, on HIGH 3 minutes; stir to blend. Stir in cottage fries and ⅔ *cup* onions. Cook, covered, 5 minutes; stir. Top with broccoli spears as above. Arrange unbrowned pork chops over broccoli *stalks* with meatiest parts toward edges of dish. Cook, covered, on MEDIUM (50-60%) 24 to 30 minutes or until pork chops are no longer pink. Turn chops over, sprinkle with seasoned salt and rotate dish halfway through cooking time. Top with remaining ⅔ *cup* onions; cook, uncovered, on HIGH 1 minute. Let stand 5 minutes.

Sweet Potato Soufflé ▶

5 tablespoons butter or
margarine, divided
1½ pounds sweet potatoes, peeled
and cut into 1-inch cubes
⅓ cup firmly packed brown sugar
¼ cup dry sherry
1 teaspoon ground cinnamon

½ teaspoon ground nutmeg
1 cup milk
3 tablespoons all-purpose flour
½ teaspoon salt
3 egg yolks
5 egg whites

1. Preheat oven to 400°F. Grease 2-quart soufflé dish with 1 tablespoon butter.

2. Place potatoes in 3-quart saucepan; add water to cover. Bring to a boil over high heat. Reduce heat to medium-low. Simmer, uncovered, 12 to 14 minutes until potatoes are fork-tender. Drain. Transfer potatoes to large bowl; mash with potato masher until smooth. Stir in sugar, sherry, cinnamon and nutmeg until well blended; set aside.

3. Heat milk in small saucepan over medium heat until warm. Melt remaining 4 tablespoons butter in 2-quart saucepan over medium heat. Reduce heat to low; stir in flour. Cook and stir 2 minutes or until completely smooth. Gradually whisk in warm milk until well blended. Add salt; whisk constantly over medium heat 2 to 3 minutes until sauce boils and thickens.

4. Whisk in egg yolks, 1 at a time, blending completely after each. Cook and stir 1 minute more. Add to potato mixture; mix well. Cool completely.

5. Meanwhile, beat egg whites in large bowl with electric mixer at high speed until stiff peaks form. Stir ⅓ beaten egg whites into cooled potato mixture with rubber spatula; fold in remaining egg whites.

6. Pour potato mixture into prepared dish, gently smoothing top with spatula. Place dish in center of oven; bake 10 minutes. *Reduce oven temperature to 375°F.* Bake 45 to 50 minutes longer until soufflé edge is puffy, center is set and top is lightly browned. Serve immediately.

Makes 6 servings

Oven-Easy Beef

4 cups frozen hash brown
    potatoes, thawed
3 tablespoons vegetable oil
⅛ teaspoon black pepper
1 pound ground beef
1 cup water
1 package (about ¾ ounce)
    brown gravy mix
½ teaspoon garlic salt

1 package (10 ounces) frozen
    mixed vegetables, thawed
    and drained
1 cup (4 ounces) shredded
    Cheddar cheese
1⅓ cups (2.8 ounce can)
    FRENCH'S® French Fried
    Onions

Preheat oven to 400°F. In 8×12-inch baking dish, combine potatoes, oil and pepper. Firmly press potato mixture evenly across bottom and up sides of dish to form a shell. Bake, uncovered, at 400°F for 15 minutes. Meanwhile, in large skillet, brown ground beef; drain. Stir in water, gravy mix and garlic salt; bring to a boil. Add mixed vegetables; reduce heat to medium and cook, uncovered, 5 minutes. Remove from heat and stir in *½ cup* cheese and *⅔ cup* French Fried Onions; spoon into hot potato shell. *Reduce oven temperature to 350°F.* Bake, uncovered, at 350°F for 15 minutes or until heated through. Top with remaining cheese and *⅔ cup* onions; bake, uncovered, 5 minutes or until onions are golden brown. *Makes 4 to 6 servings*

Pizza-Style Stuffed Potatoes ▶

½ pound lean ground American
    lamb
4 large baking potatoes,
    scrubbed
⅓ cup finely chopped onion
⅓ cup chopped green bell pepper
¼ cup chopped mushrooms
2 teaspoons dried parsley flakes
2 teaspoons Italian seasoning
½ teaspoon garlic powder

½ cup plain nonfat yogurt
½ teaspoon salt
¼ teaspoon black pepper
1 cup (4 ounces) shredded
    reduced-fat mozzarella
    cheese, divided
½ cup pizza sauce
12 sliced black olives (optional)
2 tablespoons grated Parmesan
    cheese

Pierce potatoes several times with fork. Microwave on paper towel at HIGH 10 to 12 minutes or until potatoes are soft. Cool slightly.

Preheat oven to 400°F. Cook lamb in medium skillet over medium heat until no longer pink; drain. Add onion, bell pepper and mushrooms; microwave at HIGH 2 minutes. Stir in parsley, Italian seasoning and garlic powder.

Make lengthwise slit in each potato. Scoop out pulp leaving shells intact. Place pulp in medium bowl. Beat in yogurt, salt and black pepper. Add ⅔ cup mozzarella cheese and ground lamb mixture; mix until blended. Spoon mixture into potato shells. Top each potato with pizza sauce, remaining ⅓ cup mozzarella cheese, olives, if desired, and Parmesan cheese.* Bake 20 minutes or until hot and bubbly.   *Makes 4 servings*

*Stuffed potatoes can be wrapped in foil and frozen before baking. To serve, thaw in refrigerator and bake as directed.

Nutrition per serving: *Calories: 408, Total Fat: 16 g, Cholesterol: 56 mg, Sodium: 782 mg*

Favorite recipe from **American Lamb Council**

POTATOES
in Supporting Roles

Potato side dishes are perfect co-stars for your favorite entrées. Try these satisfying casseroles, great gratins and fresh-from-the-grill accompaniments.

Fresh Vegetable Casserole ▶

8 small new potatoes, scrubbed
8 baby carrots
1 small cauliflower, broken into
    florets
4 stalks asparagus, cut into
    1-inch pieces
3 tablespoons margarine or
    butter

3 tablespoons all-purpose flour
2 cups milk
    Salt
    Black pepper
¾ cup (3 ounces) shredded
    Cheddar cheese
    Chopped fresh cilantro

Preheat oven to 350°F. Cook vegetables until crisp-tender. Arrange vegetables in greased 2-quart casserole. To make sauce, melt margarine in medium saucepan over medium heat. Stir in flour until smooth; cook 2 minutes. Gradually stir in milk. Cook until thickened, stirring constantly. Season to taste with salt and pepper. Add cheese, stirring until cheese is melted. Pour sauce over vegetables and sprinkle with cilantro. Bake 15 minutes or until heated through. *Makes 4 to 6 servings*

Potato Latkes ▶

⅔ cup EGG BEATERS® Healthy
    Real Egg Product
⅓ cup all-purpose flour
¼ cup grated onion
¼ teaspoon ground black pepper
4 large potatoes, peeled and
    shredded (about 4 cups)

3 tablespoons FLEISCHMANN'S®
    Margarine, divided
1½ cups sweetened applesauce
    Fresh chives, for garnish

In large bowl, combine Egg Beaters, flour, onion and pepper; set aside.

Pat shredded potatoes dry with paper towels. Stir into egg mixture. In large nonstick skillet, over medium-high heat, melt 1½ tablespoons margarine. For each pancake, spoon about ⅓ cup potato mixture into skillet, spreading into 4-inch circle. Cook for 3 minutes on each side or until golden; remove and keep warm. Repeat with remaining mixture, using remaining margarine as needed to make 12 pancakes. Serve hot with applesauce. Garnish with chives.

Makes 4 servings

Prep Time: 20 minutes   **Cook Time:** 18 minutes

Nutrients per serving: Calories: 460, Total Fat: 12 g, Saturated Fat: 4 g, Cholesterol: 0 mg, Sodium: 208 mg, Dietary Fiber: 4 g

Sweet Potato-Cranberry Bake

1 can (40 ounces) whole sweet
    potatoes, drained
1⅓ cups (2.8 ounce can)
    FRENCH'S® French Fried
    Onions

2 cups fresh cranberries
2 tablespoons packed brown
    sugar
⅓ cup honey

Preheat oven to 400°F. In 1½-quart casserole, layer sweet potatoes, ⅔ *cup* French Fried Onions and *1 cup* cranberries. Sprinkle with brown sugar; drizzle with *half* the honey. Top with remaining cranberries and honey. Bake, covered, at 400° for 35 minutes or until heated through. Gently stir casserole. Top with remaining ⅔ *cup* onions; bake, uncovered, 1 to 3 minutes or until onions are golden brown.

Makes 4 to 6 servings

Zippy Scalloped Potatoes ▼

Nonstick cooking spray
3 large baking potatoes (about
    2½ pounds)
1 jar (11.5 ounces) GUILTLESS
    GOURMET® Nacho Dip (mild
    or spicy)

¾ cup skim milk
Fresh cilantro leaves and red
    pepper strips (optional)

MICROWAVE DIRECTIONS: Preheat oven to 350°F. Coat microwave-safe 2-quart rectangular dish or round casserole with cooking spray. Scrub potatoes with vegetable brush; thinly slice potatoes. (Slice in food processor, if desired.) Layer in prepared dish. Cover with vented plastic wrap or lid; microwave on HIGH (100% power) 10 minutes or until potatoes are fork-tender.

Combine nacho dip and milk in 4-cup glass measure; microwave on HIGH 2 minutes. Pour over potatoes; gently stir to coat potato slices. Cover and bake 30 minutes. Uncover; bake 10 minutes more or until heated through. Let stand 5 minutes before serving. Garnish with cilantro and pepper, if desired.
Makes 8 servings

Nutrients per serving: *Calories: 184, Total Fat: trace, Saturated Fat: 0 g, Cholesterol: 0 mg, Sodium: 240 mg, Protein: 5 g, Dietary Fiber: 3 g*

As Good As Mashed Potatoes
(but Fat Free!)

4 medium IDAHO® Potatoes
   (about 1½ pounds)
1¼ cups water
4 cloves garlic, minced
4 tablespoons parsley, chopped
3 dashes hot pepper sauce

1 teaspoon salt
¼ cup nonfat sour cream
2 teaspoons prepared
   horseradish
2 teaspoons grainy mustard
1 teaspoon yellow mustard

Peel potatoes, if desired. Cut into 1-inch cubes; place in medium saucepan. Add water, garlic, parsley, pepper sauce and salt. Bring to a boil over medium-high heat. Reduce heat to low. Cover and cook about 20 minutes, stirring and breaking potatoes up with fork, adding hot water if potatoes are too dry. Continue stirring and mashing potatoes for about 5 minutes until water is absorbed and potatoes are soft and lumpy. Remove from heat, stir in the sour cream, horseradish and mustards. *Makes 4 to 6 servings*

Nutrients per serving: Calories: 110, Total Fat: 0 g, Cholesterol: 0 mg, Sodium: 447 mg, Protein: 3 g

*Favorite recipe from **Idaho® Potato***

Herb Roasted Potatoes

½ cup MIRACLE WHIP® or
   MIRACLE WHIP LIGHT®
   Dressing
1 tablespoon *each* dried
   rosemary, garlic powder and
   onion powder

1 teaspoon seasoned salt
1 tablespoon water
2 pound small red potatoes,
   quartered

MIX dressing, seasonings and water in large bowl. Add potatoes; toss to coat. Place potatoes on greased cookie sheet.

BAKE at 400°F for 30 to 40 minutes or until golden brown, stirring after 15 minutes.
Makes 8 servings

Note: Substitute dried oregano leaves for dried rosemary, if desired.

Prep Time: 15 minutes   **Baking Time:** 40 minutes

Savory Grilled Potatoes in Foil ▶

½ cup MIRACLE WHIP® Salad
    Dressing
3 garlic cloves, minced
½ teaspoon paprika

¼ teaspoon *each*: salt, pepper
3 baking potatoes, cut into
    ¼-inch slices
1 large onion, sliced

MIX salad dressing and seasonings in large bowl until well blended. Stir in potatoes and onions to coat.

DIVIDE potato mixture evenly among six 12-inch square pieces of heavy-duty foil. Seal each to form packet.

PLACE foil packets on grill over medium-hot coals (coals will have slight glow). Grill, covered, 25 to 30 minutes or until potatoes are tender.

Makes 6 side-dish servings

Prep Time: 15 minutes   **Grilling Time:** 30 minutes

Sautéed Garlic Potatoes

2 pounds boiling potatoes,
    peeled and cut into 1-inch
    pieces
3 tablespoons FILIPPO BERIO®
    Olive Oil
6 cloves garlic, skins on
1 tablespoon lemon juice

1 tablespoon chopped fresh
    chives
1 tablespoon chopped fresh
    parsley
Salt and freshly ground black
    pepper

Place potatoes in large colander; rinse under cold running water. Drain well; pat dry. In large nonstick skillet, heat olive oil over medium heat until hot. Add potatoes in a single layer. Cook, stirring and turning frequently, 10 minutes or until golden brown. Add garlic. Cover; reduce heat to low and cook very gently, shaking pan and stirring mixture occasionally, 15 to 20 minutes or until potatoes are tender when pierced with fork. Remove garlic; discard skins. In small bowl, crush garlic; stir in lemon juice. Add to potatoes; mix well. Cook 1 to 2 minutes or until heated through. Transfer to serving dish; sprinkle with chives and parsley. Season to taste with salt and pepper.

Makes 4 servings

Potato Gnocchi with Tomato Sauce ▶

2 pounds baking potatoes,
    scrubbed (3 or 4 large)
Tomato Sauce (recipe follows)
    or bottled meatless spaghetti
    sauce
⅔ to 1 cup all-purpose flour,
    divided
1 egg yolk

½ teaspoon salt
⅛ teaspoon ground nutmeg
    (optional)
Freshly grated Parmesan
    cheese
Fresh basil leaves for garnish
    (optional)

1. Preheat oven to 425°F. Pierce potatoes several times with fork. Bake 1 hour or until soft. While potatoes are baking, prepare Tomato Sauce; set aside.

2. Cut baked potatoes in half lengthwise; cool slightly. Scoop pulp from skins with spoon into medium bowl; discard skins. Mash potatoes until smooth. Add ⅓ cup flour, egg yolk, salt and nutmeg, if desired, to potato pulp; mix well to form dough.

3. Turn out dough onto well floured surface. Knead in enough remaining flour to form smooth dough that is not sticky. Divide dough into 4 equal portions. Roll each portion with hands on lightly floured surface into long, ¾- to 1-inch-wide rope. Cut each rope into 1-inch pieces; gently press thumb into center of each piece to make indentation. Space gnocchi slightly apart on lightly floured kitchen towel to prevent them from sticking together.

4. Bring 4 quarts salted water to a gentle boil in Dutch oven over high heat. To test gnocchi cooking time, drop several gnocchi into water; cook 1 minute or until gnocchi float to surface. Remove from water with slotted spoon and taste for doneness. (If gnocchi start to dissolve, shorten cooking time by several seconds.) Cook remaining gnocchi in batches, removing with slotted spoon to warm serving dish.

5. Serve gnocchi immediately topped with warm Tomato Sauce and sprinkled with cheese. Garnish with basil, if desired.   *Makes 4 servings*

Tomato Sauce

- - - - - - - - - - - - - - -

2 tablespoons olive oil or butter
1 clove garlic, minced
2 pounds ripe plum tomatoes,
    peeled, seeded and chopped
1 teaspoon sugar

¼ cup finely chopped prosciutto
    or cooked ham (optional)
1 tablespoon finely chopped
    fresh basil
Salt and black pepper to taste

1. Heat oil in medium saucepan over medium heat until hot. Add garlic; cook 30 seconds or until fragrant. Stir in tomatoes and sugar. Cook 10 minutes or until most of liquid has evaporated. Stir in prosciutto, if desired, and basil. Cook 2 minutes. Season to taste with salt and pepper.

Makes about 2 cups

Potato Gorgonzola Gratin

3 large Colorado russet potatoes, unpeeled and thinly sliced
Salt and black pepper
Ground nutmeg
½ medium onion, thinly sliced
1 medium tart green apple,* such as Granny Smith or Pippin, unpeeled, cored and thinly sliced

1 cup low-fat milk or half-and-half
3 ounces Gorgonzola or other blue cheese, crumbled
2 tablespoons grated Parmesan cheese

Preheat oven to 400°F. Arrange ½ of potatoes in 8- or 9-inch square baking dish. Season to taste with salt and pepper; sprinkle lightly with nutmeg. Top with onion and apple slices. Arrange remaining potatoes on top. Season to taste with additional salt and pepper. Pour milk over potato mixture. Cover dish with foil. Bake 30 to 40 minutes or until potatoes are tender. Remove foil; top with cheeses. Bake uncovered 10 to 15 minutes or until top is lightly brown in spots. *Makes 4 to 6 servings*

*Substitute 1 medium pear for apple, if desired.

Nutrients per serving *(¼ of recipe): Calories: 153, Total Fat: 6 g, Cholesterol: 15 mg, Sodium: 254 mg, Protein: 7 g, Dietary Fiber: 2 g*

*Favorite recipe from **Colorado Potato Administrative Committee***

Salsa Topped Baked Potatoes

4 large baking potatoes
2 tablespoons olive oil
1 large onion, diced
1 medium zucchini, diced
1 medium yellow squash, diced
2 large cloves garlic, minced
3 cups chopped ripe tomatoes (about 2 large)

¼ cup fresh basil
2 tablespoons red wine vinegar
1½ teaspoons TABASCO® brand Pepper Sauce
½ teaspoon salt

Preheat oven to 450°F. Pierce potatoes several times with fork. Place in shallow baking pan. Bake 45 minutes or until soft.

Meanwhile, to prepare salsa, heat oil in large skillet over medium heat. Add onion; cook and stir 5 minutes. Add zucchini, yellow squash and garlic; cook 3 minutes. Add tomatoes, basil, vinegar, TABASCO® Sauce and salt. Bring to a boil over high heat. Reduce heat to low. Simmer, uncovered, 5 minutes to blend flavors, stirring occasionally. Cut lengthwise slit in potatoes. Top with warm salsa. *Makes 4 servings*

Double-Baked Potatoes

3 large baking potatoes, scrubbed
¼ cup skim milk, warmed
1 cup (4 ounces) shredded reduced-fat Cheddar cheese
¾ cup whole kernel corn
1 tablespoon finely chopped fresh oregano *or* ½ teaspoon dried oregano leaves

½ teaspoon chili powder
Nonstick cooking spray
1 cup chopped onion
½ to 1 cup chopped poblano peppers
3 cloves garlic, minced
½ teaspoon salt
¼ teaspoon black pepper
3 tablespoons chopped fresh cilantro

1. Preheat oven to 400°F. Pierce potatoes several times with fork. Wrap each potato in foil. Bake about 1 hour or until soft. Cool slightly. *Reduce oven temperature to 350°F.*

2. Cut potatoes in half lengthwise; scoop out pulp with spoon leaving ¼-inch shells. Set shells aside. Beat potatoes in large bowl with electric mixer until coarsely mashed. Add milk; beat until smooth. Stir in cheese, corn, oregano and chili powder. Set aside.

3. Spray medium skillet with nonstick cooking spray. Add onion, poblano peppers and garlic; cook and stir 5 to 8 minutes or until tender. Stir in salt and black pepper.

4. Spoon potato mixture into potato shells. Sprinkle with onion mixture. Place stuffed potatoes in small baking pan. Bake 20 to 30 minutes or until heated through. Sprinkle with cilantro. *Makes 6 servings*

Nutrients per serving: Calories: 176, Total Fat: 3 g, Saturated Fat: 1 g, Cholesterol: 10 mg, Sodium: 451 mg, Protein: 7 g, Dietary Fiber: 1 g

Sweet Potato Gratin ▶

3 pounds sweet potatoes, scrubbed (about 4 to 5 large)

½ cup margarine or butter, divided

¼ cup plus 2 tablespoons packed light brown sugar, divided

2 eggs

⅔ cup orange juice

2 teaspoons ground cinnamon, divided

½ teaspoon salt

¼ teaspoon ground nutmeg

⅓ cup all-purpose flour

¼ cup uncooked old-fashioned oats

⅓ cup chopped pecans or walnuts

1. Preheat oven to 350°F. Pierce potatoes several times with fork. Bake potatoes 1 hour or until soft. Or, microwave at HIGH 16 to 18 minutes, rotating and turning over after 9 minutes. Let stand 5 minutes.

2. Cut potatoes lengthwise into halves. Scrape pulp from skins into large bowl; discard skins. Beat ¼ cup margarine and 2 tablespoons sugar into potatoes with electric mixer at medium speed until margarine is melted. Beat in eggs, orange juice, 1½ teaspoons cinnamon, salt and nutmeg until smooth. Pour mixture into 1½-quart baking dish or gratin dish; smooth top.

3. For topping, combine flour, oats, remaining ¼ cup sugar and remaining ½ teaspoon cinnamon in medium bowl. Cut in remaining ¼ cup margarine with pastry blender or 2 knives until mixture becomes coarse crumbs. Stir in pecans. Sprinkle topping evenly over potato mixture.

4. Bake 25 to 30 minutes in 350°F oven or until heated through. For crisper topping, broil 5 inches from heat 2 to 3 minutes or until golden brown.

Makes 6 to 8 servings

Note: Gratin may be prepared a day ahead. Complete through step 3, cover and refrigerate.

Grilled Cajun Potato Wedges ▶

3 large baking potatoes,
    scrubbed (about 2 pounds)
¼ cup olive oil
2 cloves garlic, minced
1 teaspoon salt
1 teaspoon paprika

½ teaspoon dried thyme leaves
½ teaspoon dried oregano leaves
¼ teaspoon black pepper
⅛ to ¼ teaspoon ground red
    pepper

Prepare grill. Preheat oven to 425°F. Meanwhile, cut potatoes in half lengthwise, then cut each half lengthwise into 4 wedges. Place potatoes in large bowl. Add oil and garlic; toss to coat well. Combine salt, paprika, thyme, oregano, black pepper and red pepper in small bowl. Sprinkle over potatoes; toss to coat well. Place potato wedges in single layer in shallow roasting pan. (Reserve remaining oil mixture left in large bowl.) Bake 20 minutes. Meanwhile, cover 2 cups mesquite chips with cold water; soak 20 minutes.

Drain mesquite chips; sprinkle over coals. Place potato wedges on their sides on grid. Grill on covered grill over medium coals 15 to 20 minutes or until potatoes are brown and fork-tender, brushing with reserved oil mixture halfway through grilling time and turning once. *Makes 4 to 6 side-dish servings*

New Potatoes with Crushed Red Peppers

1½ tablespoons BERTOLLI® Extra
    Virgin or Classico Olive Oil
2 pounds small red new
    potatoes, rinsed and
    quartered

½ teaspoon crushed hot red
    pepper
Salt and freshly ground black
    pepper

1. Heat oil in nonstick skillet until hot enough to sizzle when piece of potato added. Add potatoes; turn the heat to medium-high and cook the potatoes, turning often, until evenly browned.

2. Sprinkle with the crushed red pepper; cover and cook until the potatoes are tender, about 10 minutes. Sprinkle with salt and pepper. *Makes 4 servings*

Nutrients per serving: Calories: 229, Total Fat: 6 g, Saturated Fat: 1 g, Monounsaturated Fat: 4 g, Cholesterol: 0 mg, Sodium: 18 mg, Protein: 4 g, Dietary Fiber: 4 g

RISE & SHINE
Brunch Dishes

Potatoes have always been a popular accompaniment to breakfast eggs. Now discover how they can add excitement to brunch dishes, such as omelets, frittatas, quiches and quick breads.

Potato-Carrot Pancakes ▶

1 pound baking potatoes, peeled
   (3 medium)
1 medium carrot
2 tablespoons minced green
   onion

1 tablespoon all-purpose flour
1 egg, beaten
½ teaspoon salt
⅛ teaspoon black pepper
2 tablespoons vegetable oil

1. Shred potatoes and carrot. Wrap in several thicknesses of paper towels; squeeze to remove excess moisture. Place potatoes, carrot, onion, flour, egg, salt and pepper in medium bowl; mix well.

2. Heat oil in large skillet over medium heat. Drop spoonfuls of potato mixture into skillet; flatten to form thin pancakes. Cook 5 minutes or until browned on bottom; turn pancakes and cook 5 minutes or until potatoes are tender.

Makes about 12 pancakes

Roasted Vegetable Omelet with Fresh Salsa ▶

Fresh Salsa (recipe follows)
4 small red-skinned potatoes, scrubbed and quartered
⅓ cup coarsely chopped red bell pepper
2 slices bacon, chopped
1 medium green onion, thinly sliced

3 eggs
Salt and black pepper to taste
1 tablespoon margarine or butter
⅓ cup shredded Colby cheese
Fresh cilantro sprigs for garnish

1. Prepare Fresh Salsa. Preheat oven to 425°F. Grease 15×10-inch jelly-roll pan.

2. Combine potatoes, bell pepper, bacon and green onion in prepared pan. Bake 30 minutes or until potatoes are tender, stirring occasionally.

3. Beat eggs, 1 tablespoon water, salt and black pepper in small bowl. Melt margarine in 10-inch skillet over medium-high heat. Pour egg mixture into skillet; cook until eggs begin to set. Gently lift sides of omelet with spatula to allow liquid to run underneath.

4. When omelet is set but not dry and bottom is lightly browned, remove from heat. Place roasted vegetable mixture over half of omelet; sprinkle with cheese. Gently fold omelet in half. Transfer to serving plate. Serve warm with Fresh Salsa. Garnish, if desired.

Makes 2 servings

Fresh Salsa

3 medium plum tomatoes, seeded and chopped
2 tablespoons chopped onion
1 small jalapeño pepper, seeded and minced*

1 tablespoon chopped fresh cilantro
1 tablespoon lime juice
¼ teaspoon salt
⅛ teaspoon black pepper

Stir together tomatoes, onion, jalapeño pepper, cilantro, lime juice, salt and black pepper. Refrigerate until ready to serve.

*Jalapeño peppers can sting and irritate the skin; wear rubber gloves when handling peppers and do not touch eyes. Wash hands after handling.

Guido's Omelet

1 cup FRANK'S or SNOWFLOSS
    Italian Style Diced Tomatoes,
    drained
12 ounces bulk sausage
1 cup diced potatoes
1 medium onion, chopped

⅓ cup diced green bell pepper
1 tablespoon Worcestershire
    sauce
Butter or nonstick cooking
    spray
6 eggs, beaten

1. Crumble sausage in skillet. Brown over medium-high heat. Drain well.

2. Reduce heat to medium; add tomatoes, potatoes, onion, pepper and Worcestershire sauce. Cook uncovered 3 to 4 minutes. Remove from heat.

3. Coat 10-inch skillet with butter; heat over medium heat. Pour eggs into skillet. Cook until eggs are set on the bottom.

4. Spread sausage mixture evenly over eggs. Cover and cook 2 to 3 minutes or until top is set. Fold omelet in half or thirds. *Makes 2 servings*

Prep Time: 15 minutes   **Cook Time:** 10 minutes

Potato Parmesan Muffins

1 medium Colorado potato,
    peeled and coarsely chopped
Milk
1⅔ cups all-purpose flour
3 to 4 tablespoons grated
    Parmesan cheese, divided
3 tablespoons sugar

2 teaspoons baking powder
½ teaspoon dried basil leaves,
    crushed
¼ teaspoon baking soda
¼ cup vegetable oil
1 egg, beaten

Preheat oven at 400°F. Grease 10 muffin cups or line muffin cups with paper baking cups. Place potato and ½ cup water in small saucepan. Bring to a boil over high heat. Reduce heat to low. Cook, covered, 10 minutes or until tender. (Do not drain.) Mash potato until smooth or place mixture in blender container and blend until smooth. Place in 1-cup measure; add milk to measure 1 cup.

Combine flour, 2 tablespoons Parmesan cheese, sugar, baking powder, basil and soda in large bowl. Combine potato mixture, oil and egg in small bowl; add all at once to flour mixture. Stir just until dry ingredients are moistened. Spoon batter into prepared muffin cups. Sprinkle tops with remaining 1 to 2 tablespoons Parmesan cheese. Bake 20 minutes or until lightly browned. Remove from pan and cool on wire rack.

Makes 10 muffins

Nutrients per serving *(1 muffin): Calories: 170, Total Fat: 7 g, Cholesterol: 23 mg, Sodium: 174 mg, Protein: 4 g, Dietary Fiber: 1 g*

Favorite recipe of **Colorado Potato Administrative Committee**

Potato and Apple Sauté

2 medium baking potatoes, peeled and diced
4 strips bacon, diced
3 tablespoons olive oil
½ cup BLUE DIAMOND® Chopped Natural Almonds
1 cup chopped onion
1 small, tart green apple, peeled, cored and diced
1 teaspoon sugar
½ teaspoon salt
1 teaspoon black pepper

Cook potatoes in salted, boiling water until barely tender. Drain and set aside. Sauté bacon in oil in medium skillet over medium heat until soft and translucent. Add almonds; sauté until almonds are crisp. Remove bacon and almonds with slotted spoon to paper towels to drain.

In fat remaining in pan, sauté onion until translucent. Add potatoes and sauté until potatoes and onion begin to brown. Add apple and continue to cook until apple is tender but still hold its shape. Return bacon and almonds to pan. Sprinkle with sugar and salt. Sauté 1 to 2 minutes longer until sugar dissolves. Stir in pepper.

Makes 4 to 6 servings

Farmstand Frittata ▶

Nonstick cooking spray
½ cup chopped onion
1 medium red bell pepper, cut
    into thin strips
1 cup cooked quartered
    unpeeled red-skinned
    potatoes
1 cup broccoli florets, blanched
    and drained

6 egg whites
1 cup cholesterol-free egg
    substitute
1 tablespoon chopped fresh
    parsley
½ teaspoon salt
¼ teaspoon black pepper
½ cup (2 ounces) shredded
    reduced-fat Cheddar cheese

1. Spray large nonstick ovenproof skillet with cooking spray; heat over medium heat until hot. Add onion and bell pepper; cook and stir 3 minutes or until crisp-tender. Add potatoes and broccoli; cook and stir 1 to 2 minutes or until heated through.

2. Whisk together egg whites, egg substitute, parsley, salt and black pepper in medium bowl.

3. Spread vegetables in even layer in skillet. Pour egg white mixture over vegetables; cover and cook over medium heat 10 to 12 minutes or until egg mixture is set.

4. Meanwhile, preheat broiler. Top frittata with cheese. Broil, 4 inches from heat, 1 minute or until cheese is bubbly and golden brown. Cut into wedges.

Makes 5 servings

Nutrients per serving: Calories: 143, Total Fat: 2 g, Saturated Fat: 1 g, Cholesterol: 8 mg, Sodium: 459 mg, Protein: 14 g, Dietary Fiber: 3 g

San Juan Quiche

1 sheet frozen puff pastry, thawed
3 medium Colorado potatoes, thinly sliced
4 slices bacon, cooked and drained
1 cup (4 ounces) shredded Gruyère cheese
4 eggs, beaten
1 cup light cream or half-and-half
½ cup soft bread crumbs
¼ cup shredded Asiago cheese

Preheat oven to 375°F. Roll out pastry sheet to 13-inch round; carefully press pastry onto bottom and up side of quiche dish. Prick bottom of dish with fork. Bake 12 to 15 minutes or until golden brown. Remove from oven.

Meanwhile, place potatoes in medium saucepan. Cover with salted water. Bring to a boil over high heat. Reduce heat to low. Simmer 6 to 8 minutes or until potatoes are just tender; drain. Crumble bacon; spinkle evenly over pastry. Top with potato slices and Gruyère cheese. Combine eggs and cream in medium bowl; pour over potatoes. Combine bread crumbs and Asiago cheese; sprinkle over potato mixture. Bake 30 to 40 minutes or until nearly set in center. Let stand 5 minutes. Cut into wedges.

Makes 6 servings

Nutrients per serving: Calories: 452, Total Fat: 29 g, Cholesterol: 186 mg, Sodium: 575 mg, Protein: 17 g, Dietary Fiber: 1 g

*Favorite recipe from **Colorado Potato Administrative Committee***

Sweet Potato Biscuits ▶

2½ cups all-purpose flour
¼ cup packed brown sugar
1 tablespoon baking powder
¾ teaspoon salt
¾ teaspoon ground cinnamon
¼ teaspoon ground ginger
¼ teaspoon ground allspice
½ cup shortening
½ cup chopped pecans
¾ cup mashed canned sweet potatoes
½ cup milk

1. Preheat oven to 450°F.

2. Combine flour, sugar, baking powder, salt, cinnamon, ginger and allspice in medium bowl. Cut in shortening with pastry blender or 2 knives until mixture resembles coarse crumbs. Stir in pecans.

3. Combine sweet potatoes and milk in medium bowl with wire whisk until smooth. Make well in center of dry ingredients. Add sweet potato mixture; stir until mixture forms soft dough that clings together and forms a ball.

4. Turn out dough onto well floured surface. Knead dough gently 10 to 12 times. Roll or pat dough to ½-inch thickness. Cut out dough with floured 2½-inch biscuit cutter.

5. Place biscuits 2 inches apart on *ungreased* baking sheet. Bake 12 to 14 minutes or until tops and bottoms are golden brown. Serve warm.   *Makes about 12 biscuits*

Potato Breakfast Custard

3 large Colorado russet variety
    potatoes, peeled and thinly
    sliced
  Salt and black pepper
8 ounces low-fat bulk sausage,
    cooked and crumbled*
⅓ cup roasted red pepper, thinly
    sliced *or* 1 jar (2 ounces)
    sliced pimientos, drained

3 eggs
1 cup low-fat milk
3 tablespoons chopped chives or
    green onion tops
¾ teaspoon dried thyme or
    oregano leaves, crushed
  Salsa and sour cream
    (optional)

Preheat oven to 375°F. Butter 8- or 9-inch square baking dish or other small casserole. Arrange ½ of potatoes in baking dish. Season to taste with salt and black pepper. Cover with ½ of sausage. Arrange the remaining potatoes over sausage; season to taste with salt and black pepper. Top with remaining sausage and red peppers. Beat eggs, milk, chives and thyme until blended. Pour over potatoes. Cover baking dish with foil and bake 45 to 50 minutes or until potatoes are tender. Uncover and bake 5 to 10 minutes longer. Serve with salsa and sour cream, if desired.   *Makes 4 to 5 servings*

*Substitute 6 ounces finely diced lean ham or 6 ounces crumbled, cooked turkey bacon for sausage, if desired.

Nutrients per serving (¼ *of recipe): Calories: 255, Total Fat: 13 g, Cholesterol: 132 mg, Sodium: 431 mg, Protein: 13 g, Dietary Fiber: 2 g*

*Favorite recipe from **Colorado Potato Administrative Committee***

Contents

Great Starters

Onion and Pepper Calzones

 1 teaspoon vegetable oil
½ cup chopped onion
½ cup chopped green bell pepper
¼ teaspoon salt
⅛ teaspoon dried basil leaves
⅛ teaspoon dried oregano leaves
⅛ teaspoon black pepper
 1 can (12 ounces) country biscuits
    (10 biscuits)
¼ cup (1 ounce) shredded mozzarella
    cheese
½ cup prepared spaghetti or pizza
    sauce
 2 tablespoons grated Parmesan
    cheese

1. Preheat oven to 400°F. Heat oil in medium nonstick skillet over medium-high heat. Add onion and bell pepper. Cook 5 minutes, stirring occasionally. Remove from heat. Add salt, basil, oregano and black pepper; stir to combine. Cool slightly.

2. While onion mixture is cooling, flatten biscuits into 3½-inch circles about ⅛ inch thick using palm of hand.

3. Stir mozzarella cheese into onion mixture; spoon 1 teaspoonful onto each biscuit. Fold biscuits in half, covering filling. Press edges with tines of fork to seal; transfer to baking sheet.

4. Bake 10 to 12 minutes or until golden brown. While calzones are baking, place spaghetti sauce in small microwavable bowl. Cover with vented plastic wrap. Microwave on HIGH 3 minutes or until hot.

5. To serve, spoon spaghetti sauce and Parmesan cheese evenly over each calzone. Serve immediately.

Makes 10 appetizers

Prep and Cook Time: 25 minutes

Green Onion Dip

 1 package (1 ounce) HIDDEN
    VALLEY® Milk Recipe Original
    Ranch® salad dressing mix
 1 cup mayonnaise
 1 cup (½ pint) sour cream
½ cup finely chopped green onions

In medium bowl, whisk together all ingredients. Refrigerate at least 1 hour before serving. Serve with fresh vegetables, such as cauliflowerets, carrot and celery sticks, cucumber slices, tomato wedges or turnip chips.

Makes about 2½ cups dip

Onion and Pepper Calzones

The Ultimate Onion

3 cups cornstarch
1½ cups all-purpose flour
2 teaspoons garlic salt
2 teaspoons paprika
1 teaspoon salt
1 teaspoon black pepper
2 bottles (24 ounces) beer
4 to 6 Colossal onions (4 inches in diameter)
2 cups all-purpose flour
4 teaspoons paprika
2 teaspoons garlic powder
½ teaspoon black pepper
¼ teaspoon cayenne pepper
1 pint mayonnaise
1 pint sour cream
½ cup chili sauce
½ teaspoon cayenne pepper

1. Mix cornstarch, 1½ cups flour, garlic salt, paprika, salt and 1 teaspoon black pepper in large bowl. Add beer; mix well. Set aside.

2. Cut about ¾-inch off top of each onion; peel. Being careful not to cut through bottom, cut each onion into 12 to 16 wedges.

3. Soak cut onions in ice water 10 to 15 minutes. If onions do not "bloom" cut petals slightly deeper. Meanwhile, prepare seasoned flour mixture; combine 2 cups flour, 4 teaspoons paprika, garlic powder, ½ teaspoon black pepper and ¼ teaspoon cayenne pepper in large bowl; mix well.

4. Dip cut onions into seasoned flour mixture; remove excess by shaking carefully. Dip in batter; remove excess by shaking carefully. Separate "petals" to coat thoroughly with batter. (If batter begins to separate, mix thoroughly before using.)

5. Gently place one onion in fryer basket and deep-fry at 375°F 1½ minutes. Turn onion over and fry 1 to 1½ minutes or until golden brown. Drain on paper towels. Place onion upright in shallow bowl and remove about 1 inch of "petals" from center of onion. Repeat with remaining onions.

6. Prepare creamy chili sauce; combine mayonnaise, sour cream, chili sauce and ½ teaspoon cayenne pepper in large bowl. Spoon chili sauce into small cups. Place one cup in center of each warm onion; serve.   *Makes 24 servings*

Favorite recipe from **National Onion Association**

Chili con Queso

1 pound pasteurized process cheese spread, cut into cubes
1 can (10 ounces) diced tomatoes and green chiles, undrained
1 cup sliced green onions
2 teaspoons ground coriander
2 teaspoons ground cumin
¾ teaspoon hot pepper sauce
   Green onion strips (optional)
   Hot pepper slices (optional)

SLOW COOKER DIRECTIONS
Combine all ingredients *except* green onion strips and hot pepper slices in slow cooker until well blended. Cover and cook on LOW 2 to 3 hours or until hot. Garnish with green onion strips and hot pepper slices, if desired.   *Makes 3 cups dip*

The Ultimate Onion

Savory Herb-Stuffed Onions

1 zucchini, cut lengthwise into ¼-inch-thick slices
3 shiitake mushrooms
4 large sweet onions
1 plum tomato, seeded and chopped
2 tablespoons fresh bread crumbs
1 tablespoon fresh basil *or* 1 teaspoon dried basil
1 teaspoon olive oil
¼ teaspoon salt
⅛ teaspoon ground black pepper
4 teaspoons balsamic vinegar

1. Grill zucchini on uncovered grill over medium coals 4 minutes or until tender, turning once. Cool; cut into bite-sized pieces.

2. Thread mushrooms onto metal skewers. Grill on covered grill over medium coals 20 to 30 minutes or until tender. Coarsely chop; set aside.

3. Remove stem and root ends of onions, leaving peels intact. Spray onions with nonstick cooking spray; grill root-end up on covered grill over medium coals 5 minutes or until lightly charred. Remove and let stand until cool enough to handle. Peel and scoop about 1 inch of pulp from stem ends; chop for filling and set whole onions aside.

4. Combine chopped onion, mushrooms, zucchini, tomato, bread crumbs, basil, oil, salt and pepper in large bowl; mix until well blended. Spoon stuffing mixture evenly into center of each onion.

5. Place each onion on sheet of foil; sprinkle each with 1 tablespoon water. Seal; grill onion packets on covered grill over medium coals 45 to 60 minutes or until tender. Spoon 1 teaspoon vinegar over each onion before serving.

Makes 4 appetizer servings

Beef Appetizer Kabobs

1 (7-ounce) jar roasted red peppers, drained, finely chopped
½ cup A.1.® Original or A.1.® Bold & Spicy Steak Sauce
⅓ cup ketchup
¼ cup chopped fresh parsley
2 teaspoons dried oregano leaves
1 (1½-pound) beef top round steak, cut into ¾-inch cubes (about 72 cubes)
16 green onions, cut into 1-inch pieces
24 fresh mushroom caps

Soak 24 (10-inch) wooden skewers in water at least 30 minutes.

In small bowl, blend peppers, steak sauce, ketchup, parsley and oregano; reserve ½ cup for basting kabobs. Set aside remaining pepper mixture for serving with kabobs.

Alternately thread 3 steak cubes, 2 green onion pieces and 1 mushroom cap onto each skewer. Grill kabobs over medium heat or broil 6 inches from heat source 10 to 15 minutes or until steak is of desired doneness, turning and basting often with ½ cup basting sauce. Serve with remaining pepper mixture.

Makes 24 appetizers

Savory Herb-Stuffed Onions

Meat-Filled Samosas

1 cup all-purpose flour
1 cup whole-wheat flour
1¼ teaspoons salt, divided
2 tablespoons plus 2 teaspoons
    vegetable oil, divided
⅓ to ½ cup water
1 small onion, finely chopped
2 cloves garlic, minced
1 teaspoon finely chopped fresh
    ginger
¾ pound lean ground lamb or ground
    round
2 teaspoons Garam Masala* (recipe
    follows)
¾ cup frozen peas
1 small tomato, peeled, seeded and
    chopped
2 teaspoons finely chopped cilantro
1 jalapeño pepper,** seeded and
    chopped
    Additional vegetable oil for frying
    Cilantro Chutney (recipe follows)
    (optional)

Also available at specialty stores and Indian markets.

**Jalapeño peppers can sting and irritate the skin; wear rubber gloves when handling peppers and do not touch eyes. Wash hands after handling.*

Combine flours and ½ teaspoon salt in large bowl. Stir in 2 tablespoons oil with fork; mix until mixture resembles fine crumbs. Gradually stir in enough water, about ⅓ cup, until dough forms a ball and is no longer sticky. Place dough on lightly floured surface; flatten slightly. Knead dough 5 minutes or until smooth and elastic. Divide dough in half and form 2 ropes, each about 9 inches long and 1 inch thick. Wrap in plastic wrap; let stand 1 hour.

Meanwhile, heat remaining 2 teaspoons oil in large skillet over medium heat. Add onion, garlic and ginger; cook and stir 5 minutes or until onion is softened.

Crumble meat into skillet; cook 6 to 8 minutes or until browned, stirring to separate meat. Spoon off and discard fat. Stir in Garam Masala and remaining ¾ teaspoon salt. Add peas, tomato, cilantro and jalapeño to skillet; mix well. Cover and cook 5 minutes or until peas are heated through. Cool to room temperature before filling samosas.

To form samosas, divide each rope of dough into 9 equal portions. Roll each piece on lightly floured surface into 4- to 5-inch round. Keep remaining dough pieces wrapped in plastic wrap to prevent drying. Cut each round of dough in half, forming 2 semi-circles. Moisten straight edge of 1 semi-circle with water and fold in half; press moistened edges together to seal. Spread dough apart to form cone; fill with 2 teaspoons meat filling. Press meat mixture into cone, leaving ½ inch of dough above meat mixture. Moisten edges of dough and press firmly together. Place samosas on work surface and seal edges with fork.

Heat 3 to 4 inches oil in large heavy skillet over medium-high heat to 375°F on deep-fat thermometer. Cook 4 to 6 samosas at a time 3 to 4 minutes or until crisp and golden. Drain on paper towels. Serve with Cilantro Chutney, if desired.

Makes 36 samosas

Garam Masala

2 teaspoons cumin seeds
2 teaspoons whole black
    peppercorns
1½ teaspoons coriander seeds
1 teaspoon fennel seeds
¾ teaspoon whole cloves
½ teaspoon whole cardamom seeds,
    pods removed
1 cinnamon stick, broken

Preheat oven to 250°F. Combine spices in baking pan; bake 30 minutes, stirring occasionally. Transfer spices to clean coffee or spice grinder or use mortar and pestle to pulverize. Store in covered glass jar.

Cilantro Chutney

½ cup green onions, cut into ½-inch lengths
1 to 2 hot green chili peppers, seeded and coarsely chopped
2 tablespoons chopped fresh ginger
2 cloves garlic, peeled
1 cup packed cilantro leaves
2 tablespoons vegetable oil
2 tablespoons lime juice
1 teaspoon salt
1 teaspoon sugar
¼ teaspoon ground cumin

Drop green onions, chilies, ginger and garlic through feed tube of food processor with motor running. Stop machine and add cilantro, oil, lime juice, salt, sugar and cumin; process until cilantro is finely chopped.

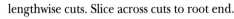

CHOPPING ONIONS

1. Peel skin from onion; cut in half through the root.

2. Make cuts parallel to cutting board, almost to root end.

3. Make vertical, lengthwise cuts. Slice across cuts to root end.

Onion and Pepper Quesadillas

1 tablespoon olive or salad oil
2 medium green bell peppers, seeded and thinly sliced
1 medium onion, thinly sliced
2 teaspoons chili powder
1 teaspoon ground cumin
1 clove garlic, minced
¼ teaspoon cayenne pepper
½ cup pitted California ripe olives, coarsely chopped
6 flour tortillas (7 to 9 inches)
¾ cup shredded Cheddar cheese
¾ cup shredded Monterey Jack cheese
Reduced-fat sour cream

Heat large skillet over medium-high heat. Add oil, bell peppers, onion, chili powder, cumin, garlic and cayenne, stirring often, until peppers and onion are soft, about 5 minutes. Remove pan from heat and stir in chopped olives; set aside. Arrange 3 tortillas in single layer on 2 baking sheets. Divide bell pepper mixture evenly among tortillas; spread to ½ inch of edges. Evenly cover with cheeses, then top each tortilla with one of remaining tortillas; press lightly. Bake at 450°F until tortillas are lightly browned, 7 to 9 minutes, switching positions of baking sheets halfway through baking. Cut each into 4 or 6 wedges. Arrange on platter and add sour cream to taste. Garnish with sliced olives.

Makes 6 servings

Prep Time: 15 minutes

Cook Time: 12 to 14 minutes

Favorite recipe from **California Olive Industry**

Cheese and Pepper Stuffed Potato Skins

6 large russet potatoes (about
  ¾ pound each), scrubbed
4 tablespoons FRANK'S® REDHOT®
  Hot Sauce, divided
2 tablespoons butter, melted
1 large red bell pepper, seeded and
  finely chopped
1 cup chopped green onions
1 cup (4 ounces) shredded Cheddar
  cheese

1. Preheat oven to 450°F. Wrap potatoes in foil; bake about 1 hour 15 minutes or until fork tender. Let stand until cool enough to handle. Cut each potato in half lengthwise; scoop out insides*, leaving a ¼-inch-thick shell. Cut shells in half crosswise. Place shells on large baking sheet.

2. Preheat broiler. Combine 1 tablespoon REDHOT sauce and butter in small bowl; brush on inside of each potato shell. Broil shells, 6 inches from heat, 8 minutes or until golden brown and crispy.

3. Combine remaining 3 tablespoons REDHOT sauce with remaining ingredients in large bowl. Spoon about 1 tablespoon mixture into each potato shell. Broil 2 minutes or until cheese melts. Cut each piece in half to serve.

Makes 12 servings

Reserve leftover potato for mashed potatoes, home-fries or soup.

Prep Time: 30 minutes

Cook Time: 1 hour 25 minutes

Savory Corn Cakes

2 cups all-purpose flour
1 teaspoon baking powder
½ teaspoon salt
2 cups frozen corn, thawed
1 cup fat-free (skim) milk
1 cup (4 ounces) shredded smoked
  Cheddar cheese
2 egg whites, beaten
1 whole egg, beaten
4 green onions, finely chopped
2 cloves garlic, minced
1 tablespoon chili powder
  Prepared salsa (optional)

1. Combine flour, baking powder and salt in large bowl with wire whisk. Stir in corn, milk, cheese, egg whites, egg, green onions, garlic and chili powder until well blended.

2. Spray large nonstick skillet with nonstick cooking spray; heat over medium-high heat.

3. Drop batter by ¼ cupfuls into skillet. Cook 3 minutes per side or until golden brown. Serve with prepared salsa.

Makes 12 cakes

*Cheese and Pepper Stuffed
Potato Skins*

Come for Brunch

Scrambled Eggs with Tomatoes & Chilies

8 eggs
½ teaspoon salt
2 tablespoons butter or margarine
2 tablespoons vegetable oil
⅓ cup finely chopped white onion
2 to 4 fresh serrano chilies, finely chopped*
2 medium tomatoes, seeded, chopped, drained
Cilantro sprigs for garnish
Warm corn tortillas (optional)
Fresh fruit (optional)

Jalapeño peppers can sting and irritate the skin; wear rubber gloves when handling peppers and do not touch eyes. Wash hands after handling.

1. Whisk eggs and salt lightly in medium bowl.

2. Heat butter and oil in large skillet over medium heat until hot. Add onion and chilies. Cook and stir 45 seconds or until hot but not soft.

3. Stir in tomatoes. Increase heat to medium-high. Cook and stir 45 seconds or until tomatoes are very hot.

4. Add egg mixture all at once to skillet. Cook without stirring 1 minute. Cook 2 to 3 minutes more, stirring lightly until eggs are softly set. Garnish, if desired. Serve with tortillas and fruit.

Makes 4 servings

Note: Fresh chilies provide crunchy texture that cannot be duplicated with canned chilies. For milder flavor, seed some or all of the chilies.

Potato & Onion Frittata

1 small baking potato, peeled, halved and sliced ⅛-inch thick (about ½ cup)
¼ cup chopped onion
1 clove garlic, minced
Dash ground black pepper
1 tablespoon FLEISCHMANN'S® Original Margarine
1 cup EGG BEATERS® Healthy Real Egg Product

In 8-inch nonstick skillet, over medium-high heat, sauté potato, onion, garlic and pepper in margarine until tender. Pour Egg Beaters evenly into skillet over potato mixture. Cook without stirring for 5 to 6 minutes or until cooked on bottom and almost set on top. Carefully turn frittata; cook for 1 to 2 minutes more or until done. Slide onto serving platter; cut into wedges to serve. *Makes 2 servings*

Prep Time: 5 minutes

Cook Time: 15 minutes

Scrambled Eggs with Tomatoes & Chilies

Onion-Zucchini Bread

1 large zucchini (¾ pound),
   shredded
2½ cups all-purpose flour*
⅓ cup grated Parmesan cheese
1⅓ cups FRENCH'S® French Fried
   Onions
1 tablespoon baking powder
1 tablespoon chopped fresh basil or
   1 teaspoon dried basil leaves
½ teaspoon salt
¾ cup milk
½ cup (1 stick) butter or margarine,
   melted
¼ cup packed light brown sugar
2 eggs

*You may substitute 1¼ cups whole-wheat flour for
1¼ cups of all-purpose flour.

Preheat oven to 350°F. Grease 9×5×3-
inch loaf pan.

Drain zucchini in colander. Combine flour,
cheese, French Fried Onions, baking
powder, basil and salt in large bowl.

Combine milk, butter, brown sugar and
eggs in medium bowl; whisk until well
blended. Place zucchini in kitchen towel;
squeeze out excess liquid. Stir zucchini
into milk mixture.

Stir milk mixture into flour mixture, stirring
just until moistened. Do not overmix.
(Batter will be very stiff and dry.) Spoon
batter into prepared pan. Run knife down
center of batter.

Bake 50 to 65 minutes or until toothpick
inserted in center comes out clean. Cool in
pan on wire rack 10 minutes. Remove
bread from pan to wire rack; cool
completely. Cut into slices to serve.**

Makes 10 to 12 servings

**For optimum flavor, wrap bread overnight and serve
the next day. Great when toasted!

Prep Time: 20 minutes

Cook Time: about 1 hour

Double Onion Quiche

3 cups thinly sliced yellow onions
3 tablespoons butter or margarine
1 cup thinly sliced green onions
3 eggs
1 cup heavy cream
½ cup grated Parmesan cheese
¼ teaspoon hot pepper sauce
1 package (1 ounce) HIDDEN
   VALLEY® Milk Recipe Original
   Ranch® salad dressing mix
1 (9-inch) deep-dish pastry shell,
   baked, cooled
Fresh oregano sprig for garnish

Preheat oven to 350°F. In medium skillet,
cook and stir yellow onions in butter,
stirring occasionally, about 10 minutes.
Add green onions; cook 5 minutes.
Remove from heat; cool.

In large bowl, whisk eggs until frothy.
Whisk in cream, cheese, pepper sauce and
salad dressing mix. Stir in cooled onion
mixture. Pour egg and onion mixture into
cooled pastry shell. Bake until top is
browned and knife inserted in center
comes out clean, 35 to 40 minutes. Cool
on wire rack 10 minutes before slicing.
Garnish with oregano.

Makes 8 servings

Onion-Zucchini Bread

Onion, Cheese and Tomato Tart

Parmesan-Pepper Dough (recipe
  follows)
1 tablespoon butter
1 medium onion, thinly sliced
1 cup (4 ounces) shredded Swiss
  cheese
2 to 3 ripe tomatoes, sliced
  Black pepper
2 tablespoons snipped fresh chives

1. Prepare Parmesan-Pepper Dough.

2. Melt butter in large skillet over medium heat. Add onion; cook and stir 20 minutes or until tender.

3. Spread onion over prepared dough. Sprinkle with cheese. Let rise in warm place 20 to 30 minutes or until edges are puffy.

4. Preheat oven to 400°F. Top dough with tomatoes. Sprinkle with pepper. Bake 25 minutes or until edges are deep golden and cheese is melted. Let cool 10 minutes. Transfer to serving platter. Sprinkle with chives. Cut into wedges.

Makes 6 to 8 servings

Parmesan-Pepper Dough

1 package (¼ ounce) active dry yeast
1 tablespoon sugar
⅔ cup warm water (105° to 115°F)
2 cups all-purpose flour, divided
¼ cup grated Parmesan cheese
1 teaspoon salt
½ teaspoon black pepper
1 tablespoon olive oil

1. Sprinkle yeast and sugar over warm water in small bowl; stir until yeast is dissolved. Let stand 5 minutes or until mixture is bubbly.

2. Combine 1¾ cups flour, cheese, salt and pepper in large bowl. Pour yeast mixture and oil over flour mixture and stir until mixture clings together.

3. Turn out dough onto lightly floured surface. Knead 8 to 10 minutes or until smooth and elastic, adding remaining ¼ cup flour if necessary. Shape dough into a ball; place in large greased bowl. Turn dough so that top is greased. Cover with towel; let rise in warm place 1 hour or until doubled in bulk.

4. Punch down dough. Knead on lightly floured surface 1 minute or until smooth. Flatten into a disc. Roll dough to make 11-inch round. Press into bottom and up side of buttered 9- or 10-inch tart pan with removable bottom.

Spicy Onion Bread

2 tablespoons instant minced onion
⅓ cup water
1½ cups biscuit mix
1 egg, slightly beaten
½ cup milk
½ teaspoon TABASCO® brand Pepper
  Sauce
2 tablespoons butter, melted
½ teaspoon caraway seeds (optional)

Preheat oven to 400°F. Soak instant minced onion in water 5 minutes. Combine biscuit mix, egg, milk and TABASCO® Sauce in large bowl and stir until blended. Stir in onion. Turn into greased 8-inch pie plate. Brush with melted butter. Sprinkle with caraway seeds. Bake 20 to 25 minutes or until golden brown. *Makes 8 servings*

Onion, Cheese and Tomato Tart

Feta Brunch Bake

1 medium red bell pepper
2 bags (10 ounces *each*) fresh
   spinach, washed and stemmed
6 eggs
6 ounces crumbled feta cheese
⅓ cup chopped onion
2 tablespoons chopped fresh parsley
¼ teaspoon dried dill weed
   Dash ground black pepper

Preheat broiler. Place bell pepper on foil-lined broiler pan. Broil, 4 inches from heat, 15 to 20 minutes or until blackened on all sides, turning every 5 minutes with tongs. Place in paper bag; close bag and set aside to cool about 15 to 20 minutes. To peel pepper, cut around core, twist and remove. Cut in half and peel off skin with paring knife; rinse under cold water to remove seeds. Cut into ½-inch pieces.

Blanch spinach; squeeze to remove excess water. Finely chop spinach.

Preheat oven to 400°F. Grease 1-quart baking dish. Beat eggs in large bowl with electric mixer at medium speed until foamy. Stir in bell pepper, spinach, cheese, onion, parsley, dill weed and black pepper. Pour egg mixture into prepared dish. Bake 20 minutes or until set. Let stand 5 minutes before serving. Garnish as desired.

Makes 4 servings

Crispy Onion Crescent Rolls

1 can (8 ounces) refrigerated
   crescent dinner rolls
1⅓ cups FRENCH'S® French Fried
   Onions, slightly crushed
1 egg, beaten

Preheat oven to 375°F. Line large baking sheet with foil. Separate refrigerated rolls into 8 triangles. Sprinkle center of each triangle with about *1½ tablespoons* French Fried Onions. Roll-up triangles from short side, jelly-roll fashion. Sprinkle any excess onions over top of crescents.

Arrange crescents on prepared baking sheet. Brush with beaten egg. Bake 15 minutes or until golden brown and crispy. Transfer to wire rack; cool slightly.

Makes 8 servings

Prep Time: 15 minutes

Cook Time: 15 minutes

ONION TIP

Eat leeks in March and ramsins
in May, and all the year after
the physicians may play.
-Old English proverb

Feta Brunch Bake

Spicy Mexican Frittata

1 fresh jalapeño pepper*
1 clove garlic
1 medium tomato, peeled, halved, seeded and quartered
½ teaspoon ground coriander
½ teaspoon chili powder
½ cup chopped onion
1 cup frozen corn
6 egg whites
2 eggs
¼ cup fat-free (skim) milk
¼ teaspoon salt
¼ teaspoon black pepper
¼ cup (1 ounce) shredded part-skim farmer or mozzarella cheese

*Jalapeño peppers can sting and irritate the skin; wear rubber gloves when handling peppers and do not touch eyes. Wash hands after handling.

Add jalapeño pepper and garlic to food processor or blender; process until finely chopped. Add tomato, coriander and chili powder. Cover; process until tomato is almost smooth.

Spray large skillet with nonstick cooking spray; heat over medium heat. Add onion to skillet; cook and stir until tender. Stir in tomato mixture and corn. Cook 3 to 4 minutes or until liquid is almost evaporated, stirring occasionally.

Combine egg whites, eggs, milk, salt and black pepper in medium bowl. Add egg mixture all at once to skillet. Cook, without stirring, 2 minutes until eggs begin to set. Run large spoon around edge of skillet, lifting eggs for even cooking. Remove skillet from heat when eggs are almost set but surface is still moist.

Sprinkle with cheese. Cover; let stand 3 to 4 minutes or until surface is set and cheese melts. Cut into wedges.

Makes 4 servings

Mushroom & Onion Egg Bake

1 tablespoon vegetable oil
4 green onions, chopped
4 ounces mushrooms, sliced
1 cup low-fat cottage cheese
1 cup sour cream
6 eggs
2 tablespoons all-purpose flour
¼ teaspoon salt
⅛ teaspoon freshly ground pepper
Dash hot pepper sauce

1. Preheat oven to 350°F. Grease shallow 1-quart baking dish.

2. Heat oil in medium skillet over medium heat. Add onions and mushrooms; cook until tender. Set aside.

3. Place cottage cheese in blender or food processor, process until almost smooth. Add sour cream, eggs, flour, salt, pepper and hot pepper sauce; process until combined. Stir in onions and mushrooms. Pour into prepared dish. Bake about 40 minutes or until knife inserted near center comes out clean.

Makes about 6 servings

Spicy Mexican Frittata

The Pasta Bowl

Creamy "Crab" Fettuccine

6 ounces uncooked fettuccine
3 tablespoons margarine or butter,
    divided
1 small onion, chopped
2 ribs celery, chopped
½ medium red bell pepper, chopped
2 cloves garlic, minced
1 cup reduced-fat sour cream
1 cup reduced-fat mayonnaise
1 cup (4 ounces) shredded sharp
    Cheddar cheese
2 tablespoons chopped fresh parsley
¼ teaspoon salt
⅛ teaspoon black pepper
1 pound imitation crabmeat sticks,
    cut into bite-size pieces
½ cup cornflake crumbs
    Fresh chives (optional)

Preheat oven to 350°F. Spray 2-quart square baking dish with nonstick cooking spray. Cook pasta according to package directions. Drain and set aside.

Meanwhile, melt 1 tablespoon margarine in large skillet over medium-high heat. Add onion, celery, bell pepper and garlic; cook and stir 2 minutes or until vegetables are tender.

Combine sour cream, mayonnaise, cheese, parsley, salt and black pepper in large bowl. Add crabmeat, pasta and vegetable mixture, stirring gently to combine. Pour into prepared dish.

Melt remaining 2 tablespoons margarine. Combine cornflake crumbs and margarine in small bowl; sprinkle over casserole.

Bake, uncovered, 30 minutes or until hot. Garnish if desired.   *Makes 6 servings*

Baked Ziti with Walnuts

1 cup uncooked ziti pasta
1 box (10 ounces) BIRDS EYE® frozen
    Peas & Pearl Onions
1 cup tomato sauce
½ cup chopped walnuts
1 tablespoon olive oil
2 tablespoons grated Parmesan
    cheese

• Preheat oven to 350°F.

• Cook ziti according to package directions; drain and set aside.

• In large bowl, combine vegetables, tomato sauce, walnuts and oil. Add ziti; toss well.

• Place mixture in 13×9-inch baking pan. Sprinkle with cheese.

• Bake 20 minutes or until heated through.   *Makes 4 servings*

Prep Time: 10 minutes

Cook Time: 20 minutes

Creamy "Crab" Fettuccine

The Pasta Bowl

Pasta with Onions and Goat Cheese

2 teaspoons olive oil
4 cups thinly sliced sweet onions
¾ cup (3 ounces) goat cheese
¼ cup fat-free (skim) milk
6 ounces uncooked baby bow tie or other small pasta
1 clove garlic, minced
2 tablespoons dry white wine or fat-free reduced-sodium chicken broth
1½ teaspoons chopped fresh sage *or* ½ teaspoon dried sage leaves
½ teaspoon salt
¼ teaspoon black pepper
2 tablespoons chopped toasted walnuts

Heat oil in large nonstick skillet over medium heat. Add onions; cook slowly until golden and caramelized, about 20 to 25 minutes, stirring occasionally.

Combine goat cheese and milk in small bowl; stir until well blended. Set aside.

Cook pasta according to package directions, omitting salt. Drain and set aside.

Add garlic to onions in skillet; cook until softened, about 3 minutes. Add wine, sage, salt and pepper; cook until moisture is evaporated. Remove from heat; add pasta and goat cheese mixture, stirring to melt cheese. Sprinkle with walnuts.

Makes 8 (½-cup) servings

Cheeseburger Macaroni

1 cup mostaccioli or elbow macaroni, uncooked
1 pound ground beef
1 medium onion, chopped
1 can (14½ ounces) DEL MONTE® Diced Tomatoes with Basil, Garlic & Oregano
¼ cup DEL MONTE® Tomato Ketchup
1 cup (4 ounces) shredded Cheddar cheese

1. Cook pasta according to package directions; drain.

2. Brown beef with onion in large skillet; drain. Season with salt and pepper, if desired. Stir in tomatoes, ketchup and pasta; heat through.

3. Top with cheese. Garnish, if desired.

Makes 4 servings

Prep Time: 8 minutes
Cook Time: 15 minutes

ONION TIP

Does chopping onions make you cry? Sometimes chilling the onions before cutting can help reduce the tearing effects.

Pasta with Onions and Goat Cheese

Come for Brunch

Spicy Mexican Frittata

1 fresh jalapeño pepper*
1 clove garlic
1 medium tomato, peeled, halved, seeded and quartered
½ teaspoon ground coriander
½ teaspoon chili powder
½ cup chopped onion
1 cup frozen corn
6 egg whites
2 eggs
¼ cup fat-free (skim) milk
¼ teaspoon salt
¼ teaspoon black pepper
¼ cup (1 ounce) shredded part-skim farmer or mozzarella cheese

*Jalapeño peppers can sting and irritate the skin; wear rubber gloves when handling peppers and do not touch eyes. Wash hands after handling.

Add jalapeño pepper and garlic to food processor or blender; process until finely chopped. Add tomato, coriander and chili powder. Cover; process until tomato is almost smooth.

Spray large skillet with nonstick cooking spray; heat over medium heat. Add onion to skillet; cook and stir until tender. Stir in tomato mixture and corn. Cook 3 to 4 minutes or until liquid is almost evaporated, stirring occasionally.

Combine egg whites, eggs, milk, salt and black pepper in medium bowl. Add egg mixture all at once to skillet. Cook, without stirring, 2 minutes until eggs begin to set. Run large spoon around edge of skillet, lifting eggs for even cooking. Remove skillet from heat when eggs are almost set but surface is still moist.

Sprinkle with cheese. Cover; let stand 3 to 4 minutes or until surface is set and cheese melts. Cut into wedges.

Makes 4 servings

Spicy Mexican Frittata

Mushroom & Onion Egg Bake

1 tablespoon vegetable oil
4 green onions, chopped
4 ounces mushrooms, sliced
1 cup low-fat cottage cheese
1 cup sour cream
6 eggs
2 tablespoons all-purpose flour
¼ teaspoon salt
⅛ teaspoon freshly ground pepper
Dash hot pepper sauce

1. Preheat oven to 350°F. Grease shallow 1-quart baking dish.

2. Heat oil in medium skillet over medium heat. Add onions and mushrooms; cook until tender. Set aside.

3. Place cottage cheese in blender or food processor; process until almost smooth. Add sour cream, eggs, flour, salt, pepper and hot pepper sauce; process until combined. Stir in onions and mushrooms. Pour into prepared dish. Bake about 40 minutes or until knife inserted near center comes out clean.

Makes about 6 servings

Beef Stroganoff Casserole

- 1 pound lean ground beef
- ¼ teaspoon salt
- ⅛ teaspoon black pepper
- 1 teaspoon vegetable oil
- 8 ounces sliced mushrooms
- 1 large onion, chopped
- 3 cloves garlic, minced
- ¼ cup dry white wine
- 1 can (10¾ ounces) condensed cream of mushroom soup, undiluted
- ½ cup sour cream
- 1 tablespoon Dijon mustard
- 4 cups cooked egg noodles
  Chopped fresh parsley (optional)

Preheat oven to 350°F. Spray 13×9-inch baking dish with nonstick cooking spray.

Place beef in large skillet; season with salt and pepper. Brown beef over medium-high heat until no longer pink, stirring to separate beef. Drain fat from skillet; set beef aside.

Heat oil in same skillet over medium-high heat until hot. Add mushrooms, onion and garlic; cook and stir 2 minutes or until onion is tender. Add wine. Reduce heat to medium-low and simmer 3 minutes. Remove from heat; stir in soup, sour cream and mustard until well combined. Return beef to skillet.

Place noodles in prepared dish. Pour beef mixture over noodles; stir until noodles are well coated.

Bake, uncovered, 30 minutes or until heated through. Sprinkle with parsley, if desired. *Makes 6 servings*

Pasta with Spinach-Cheese Sauce

- ¼ cup FILIPPO BERIO® Extra-Virgin Olive Oil, divided
- 1 medium onion, chopped
- 1 clove garlic, chopped
- 3 cups chopped fresh spinach, washed and well drained
- 1 cup low-fat ricotta or cottage cheese
- ½ cup chopped fresh parsley
- 1 teaspoon dried basil leaves
- 1 teaspoon lemon juice
- ¼ teaspoon black pepper
- ¼ teaspoon ground nutmeg
- ¾ pound uncooked spaghetti

1. Heat 3 tablespoons olive oil in large skillet over medium heat. Cook and stir onion and garlic until onion is tender.

2. Add spinach to skillet; cook 3 to 5 minutes or until spinach wilts.

3. Place spinach mixture, cheese, parsley, basil, lemon juice, pepper and nutmeg in covered blender container. Blend until smooth. Leave in blender, covered, to keep sauce warm.

4. Cook pasta according to package directions. Do not overcook. Drain pasta, reserving ¼ cup water. In large bowl, toss pasta with remaining 1 tablespoon olive oil.

5. Add reserved ¼ cup water to sauce in blender. Blend; serve over pasta.
Makes 4 servings

Beef Stroganoff Casserole

Paprika Pork with Spinach

1 pound boneless pork loin or leg
3 tablespoons all-purpose flour
3 tablespoons vegetable oil
1 cup frozen pearl onions, thawed
1 tablespoon paprika
1 can (14½ ounces) vegetable or
   chicken broth
8 ounces medium curly egg noodles,
   uncooked
1 package (10 ounces) frozen leaf
   spinach, thawed and well
   drained
½ cup sour cream

• Trim fat from pork; discard. Cut pork into 1-inch cubes. Place flour and pork in resealable plastic food storage bag; shake until well coated.

• Heat wok over high heat about 1 minute or until hot. Drizzle oil into wok and heat 30 seconds. Add pork; stir-fry about 5 minutes or until well browned on all sides. Remove pork to large bowl.

• Add onions and paprika to wok; stir-fry 1 minute. Stir in broth, noodles and pork. Cover and bring to a boil. Reduce heat to low; cook about 8 minutes or until noodles and pork are tender, stirring occasionally.

• Stir spinach into pork and noodles. Cover and cook until heated through. Add additional water if needed. Add sour cream; mix well. Transfer to serving dish. Garnish, if desired.   *Makes 4 servings*

Pasta Peperonata

Olive oil-flavored cooking spray
4 cups sliced green, red and yellow
   bell peppers (about 1 large
   pepper of *each* color)
4 cups sliced onions
3 cloves garlic, minced
1 teaspoon dried basil leaves
½ teaspoon dried marjoram leaves
   Salt and black pepper
4 ounces spaghetti or linguini,
   cooked and kept warm
4 teaspoons grated Parmesan cheese

1. Spray large skillet with cooking spray. Heat over medium heat until hot. Add bell peppers, onions, garlic, basil and marjoram; cook, covered, 8 to 10 minutes or until vegetables are wilted. Uncover; cook and stir 20 to 30 minutes or until onions are caramelized and mixture is soft and creamy. Season to taste with salt and black pepper.

2. Spoon pasta onto plates; top with peperonata and cheese.
        Makes 6 side-dish servings

ONION TIP

During the Middle Ages, onions were so valuable, they were used as rent payments and as wedding gifts.

Pasta Peperonata

Beef & Pork

Blue Cheese Burgers with Red Onion

2 pounds ground chuck
2 cloves garlic, minced
1 teaspoon salt
½ teaspoon black pepper
4 ounces blue cheese
⅓ cup coarsely chopped walnuts, toasted
1 torpedo (long) red onion *or* 2 small red onions, sliced into ⅜-inch-thick rounds
2 baguettes (each 12 inches long)
    Olive or vegetable oil

Combine beef, garlic, salt and pepper in medium bowl. Shape meat mixture into 12 oval patties. Mash cheese and blend with walnuts in small bowl. Divide cheese mixture equally; place onto centers of 6 meat patties. Top with remaining meat patties; tightly pinch edges together to seal in filling.

Oil hot grid to help prevent sticking. Grill patties and onion, if desired, on covered grill, over medium **KINGSFORD®** Briquets, 7 to 12 minutes for medium doneness, turning once. Cut baguettes into 4-inch lengths; split each piece and brush cut side with olive oil. Move cooked burgers to edge of grill to keep warm. Grill bread, oil side down, until lightly toasted. Serve burgers on toasted baguettes.

Makes 6 servings

Zesty Onion Meat Loaf

1½ pounds ground beef
1 can (10¾ ounces) condensed Italian tomato soup, divided
1⅓ cups FRENCH'S® French Fried Onions, divided
2 tablespoons FRENCH'S® Worcestershire Sauce
¾ teaspoon salt
¼ teaspoon ground pepper
1 egg

Preheat oven to 350°F. Combine beef, ⅓ cup soup, ⅔ *cup* French Fried Onions, Worcestershire, salt, pepper and egg in large bowl. Shape into 8×4-inch loaf. Place in shallow baking pan.

Bake 1 hour or until meat loaf is no longer pink in center and meat thermometer inserted in center registers 160°F. Pour off drippings; discard.

Spoon remaining soup over meat loaf. Top with remaining ⅔ *cup* onions. Bake 5 minutes or until onions are golden.

Makes 6 servings

Prep Time: 10 minutes

Cook Time: about 1 hour

Blue Cheese Burger with Red Onion

Kublai Khan's Stir-Fry with Fiery Walnuts

Fiery Walnuts (recipe follows)
1 pound boneless tender beef steak (sirloin, rib eye or top loin) or lamb sirloin
2 tablespoons KIKKOMAN® Stir-Fry Sauce
1 teaspoon cornstarch
2 large cloves garlic, minced
2 tablespoons vegetable oil, divided
1 medium onion, cut into ¾-inch chunks
2 large carrots, cut into julienne strips
1 pound fresh spinach, washed and drained
½ pound fresh mushrooms, sliced
⅓ cup KIKKOMAN® Stir-Fry Sauce

Prepare Fiery Walnuts. Cut beef across grain into thin slices, then into narrow strips. Combine 2 tablespoons stir-fry sauce, cornstarch and garlic in medium bowl; stir in beef. Heat 1 tablespoon oil in hot wok or large skillet over medium-high heat. Add beef and stir-fry 1½ minutes; remove. Heat remaining 1 tablespoon oil in same pan. Add onion; stir-fry 2 minutes. Add carrots; stir-fry 1 minute. Add spinach and mushrooms; stir-fry 2 minutes, or until spinach is wilted. Add beef and ⅓ cup stir-fry sauce; cook and stir only until beef and vegetables are coated with sauce and heated through. Remove from heat; stir in Fiery Walnuts and serve immediately.

Makes 6 servings

Fiery Walnuts: Combine 2 teaspoons vegetable oil, ¼ teaspoon ground red pepper (cayenne) and ⅛ teaspoon salt in small skillet; heat over medium heat until hot. Add ¾ cup walnut halves or large pieces. Cook, stirring, 1 minute, or until walnuts are coated. Turn out onto small baking sheet; spread out in single layer. Bake in 350°F oven 7 minutes, or until golden. Cool.

Pork Loin Roasted in Chili-Spice Sauce

1 cup chopped onion
¼ cup orange juice
2 cloves garlic
1 tablespoon cider vinegar
1½ teaspoons chili powder
¼ teaspoon dried thyme leaves
¼ teaspoon ground cumin
¼ teaspoon ground cinnamon
⅛ teaspoon ground allspice
⅛ teaspoon ground cloves
1½ pounds pork loin, fat trimmed
3 firm large bananas
2 limes
1 ripe large papaya, peeled, seeded and cubed
1 green onion, minced

Preheat oven to 350°F. Combine onion, orange juice and garlic in food processor; process until finely chopped. Pour into medium saucepan; stir in vinegar, chili powder, thyme, cumin, cinnamon, allspice and cloves. Simmer over medium-high heat about 5 minutes or until thickened. Cut ¼-inch-deep lengthwise slits down top and bottom of roast at 1½-inch intervals. Spread about 1 tablespoon spice paste over bottom; place roast in baking pan. Spread remaining 2 tablespoons spice paste over sides and top, working mixture into slits. Cover. Bake 45 minutes or until meat thermometer registers 140°F.

Remove roast from oven; increase oven temperature to 450°F. Pour off liquid; discard. Return roast to oven and bake, uncovered, 15 minutes or until spice mixture browns lightly and meat thermometer registers 150°F in center of roast. Remove from oven; tent with foil and let stand 5 minutes before slicing.

Meanwhile, spray 9-inch pie plate or cake pan with nonstick cooking spray. Peel bananas and slice diagonally into ½-inch-

thick pieces. Place in pan. Squeeze juice from 1 lime over bananas; toss to coat evenly. Cover; bake in oven while roast stands or until hot. Stir in papaya, juice of remaining lime and green onion. Serve with roast. *Makes 6 servings*

Greek Pork Stew

¼ cup olive oil
1 pork tenderloin, cut into ½-inch cubes (about 2½ pounds)
½ pound small white onions, cut into halves
3 cloves garlic, chopped
1¼ cups dry red wine
1 can (6 ounces) tomato paste
1 can (14½ ounces) ready-to-serve beef broth
2 tablespoons balsamic vinegar or red wine vinegar
2 bay leaves
1½ teaspoons ground cinnamon
⅛ teaspoon ground coriander
Hot cooked rice (optional)

Heat oil in 5-quart Dutch oven over medium-high heat. Brown half of pork in Dutch oven. Remove with slotted spoon; set aside. Brown remaining pork. Remove with slotted spoon; set aside.

Add onions and garlic to Dutch oven. Cook and stir about 5 minutes or until onion is soft. Return pork to Dutch oven.

Combine wine and tomato paste in small bowl until blended; add to pork. Stir in broth, vinegar, bay leaves, cinnamon and coriander. Bring to a boil over high heat. Reduce heat to low. Cover and simmer 45 minutes or until pork is fork-tender. Remove bay leaves before serving. Serve with rice. *Makes 6 to 8 servings*

Stuffed Salisbury Steak with Mushroom & Onion Topping

2 pounds ground beef
¼ cup FRENCH'S® Worcestershire Sauce
2⅔ cups FRENCH'S® French Fried Onions, divided
1 teaspoon garlic salt
½ teaspoon ground black pepper
4 ounces Cheddar cheese, cut into 6 sticks (about 2×½×½ inches)
Mushroom Topping (recipe follows)

Combine beef, Worcestershire, 1⅓ cups French Fried Onions, garlic salt and pepper. Divide meat evenly into 6 portions. Place 1 stick cheese in center of each portion, firmly pressing and shaping meat into ovals around cheese.

Place steaks on grid. Grill over medium-high coals 15 minutes or until meat thermometer inserted into beef reaches 160°F, turning once. Serve with Mushroom Topping and sprinkle with remaining 1⅓ cups onions.
Makes 6 servings

Mushroom Topping

2 tablespoons butter or margarine
1 package (12 ounces) mushrooms, wiped clean and quartered
2 tablespoons FRENCH'S® Worcestershire Sauce

Melt butter in large skillet over medium-high heat. Add mushrooms; cook 5 minutes or until browned, stirring often. Add Worcestershire. Reduce heat to low. Cook 5 minutes, stirring occasionally.
Makes 6 servings

Prep Time: 25 minutes
Cook Time: 25 minutes

Swedish Meatballs

1½ cups fresh bread crumbs
1 cup heavy cream
2 tablespoons butter or margarine, divided
1 small onion, chopped
1 pound ground beef
½ pound ground pork
3 tablespoons chopped fresh parsley, divided
1½ teaspoons salt
¼ teaspoon black pepper
¼ teaspoon ground allspice
1 cup beef broth
1 cup sour cream
1 tablespoon all-purpose flour

Combine bread crumbs and cream in small bowl; mix well. Let stand 10 minutes. Melt 1 tablespoon butter in large skillet over medium heat. Add onion. Cook and stir 5 minutes or until onion is tender. Combine beef, pork, bread crumb mixture, onion, 2 tablespoons parsley, salt, pepper and allspice in large bowl; mix well. Cover; refrigerate 1 hour.

Shape meat mixture into 1-inch-thick square on cutting board. Cut into 36 squares. Shape each square into a ball. Melt remaining 1 tablespoon butter in same large skillet over medium heat. Add meatballs. Cook 10 minutes or until browned on all sides and no longer pink in center. Remove meatballs from skillet; drain on paper towels.

Drain drippings from skillet; discard. Pour broth into skillet. Heat over medium-high heat, stirring frequently and scraping up any browned bits. Reduce heat to low.

Combine sour cream and flour; mix well. Stir sour cream mixture into skillet. Cook 5 minutes, stirring constantly. Do not boil. Add meatballs. Cook 5 minutes more. Sprinkle with remaining 1 tablespoon parsley. Garnish as desired.

Makes 5 to 6 servings

Ham, Pepper & Onion Pizza with Two Cheeses

1 package pizza dough mix *or* 1 prepared (14-inch) pizza crust
3 cloves garlic, minced
½ cup extra-virgin olive oil, divided
2 cups chopped plum tomatoes
1½ cups prepared barbecue sauce
¼ cup dried oregano leaves
3 cups (12 ounces) shredded mozzarella cheese
1 cup freshly grated Parmesan cheese
2 pounds HILLSHIRE FARM® Ham, cut into strips
1 red onion, thinly sliced
1 green bell pepper, thinly sliced
1 tablespoon pine nuts (optional)

Preheat oven to 425°F. Prepare pizza dough according to package directions; spread dough onto 14-inch round baking sheet. (If using prepared crust, place crust on baking sheet.)

Sauté garlic in ¼ cup oil 5 minutes in medium saucepan over medium heat. Add tomatoes, barbecue sauce and oregano. Bring to a gentle boil; reduce heat to medium. Simmer 20 to 30 minutes or until sauce is thickened.

Brush pizza dough with 2 tablespoons oil. Cover dough with cheeses, leaving ½-inch border around edge. Cover cheese with barbecue sauce mixture; arrange Ham, onion and pepper over sauce. Drizzle pizza with remaining 2 tablespoons oil; sprinkle with pine nuts, if desired. Bake 20 minutes. Slice and serve.

Makes 4 servings

Swedish Meatballs

Thai Pork Burritos

1 pound lean ground pork
2 tablespoons grated fresh ginger
    root
1 garlic clove, peeled and crushed
2 cups coleslaw mix with carrots
1 small onion, thinly sliced
3 tablespoons soy sauce
2 tablespoons lime juice
1 tablespoon honey
2 teaspoons ground coriander
1 teaspoon sesame oil
½ teaspoon crushed red pepper
4 large (10-inch) flour tortillas,
    warmed
    Fresh cilantro, chopped (optional)

Heat large nonstick skillet over high heat. Add pork; cook and stir until pork is no longer pink, 3 to 4 minutes. Stir in ginger and garlic. Add coleslaw mix and onion and stir-fry with pork for 2 minutes, until vegetables are wilted. Combine all remaining ingredients except tortillas and cilantro in small bowl and add to skillet. Stir constantly to blend well, about 1 minute. Spoon equal portions of mixture onto warm flour tortillas and garnish with cilantro, if desired. Roll up to enclose filling and serve. *Makes 4 servings*

Prep Time: 15 minutes

Favorite recipe from **National Pork Producers Council**

Onion & Pepper Cheesesteaks

2 medium onions, thinly sliced
1 cup red, yellow and/or green bell
    pepper strips
2 tablespoons margarine or butter
½ cup GREY POUPON® Dijon
    Mustard, divided
1 tablespoon honey
4 (6- to 8-inch) steak rolls
8 frozen sandwich steaks, cooked
1 cup shredded Cheddar cheese
    (4 ounces)

In large skillet, over medium-high heat, sauté onions and bell pepper in margarine until tender. Stir in 6 tablespoons mustard and honey; reduce heat and cook 2 minutes. Keep warm.

Cut rolls in half lengthwise, not cutting completely through rolls; brush cut sides of rolls with remaining mustard. Broil rolls, cut-sides up, until golden. Top each roll with cooked steaks, onion mixture and cheese. Broil for 1 minute more or until cheese melts. Close sandwiches and serve immediately. *Makes 4 servings*

Onion & Pepper Cheesesteak

Sausage, Peppers & Onions with Grilled Polenta

5 cups canned chicken broth
1½ cups Italian polenta or yellow
    cornmeal
1½ cups cooked fresh corn or thawed
    frozen corn
2 tablespoons butter or margarine
1 cup (4 ounces) freshly grated
    Parmesan cheese
6 Italian-style sausages
2 small to medium red onions, sliced
    into rounds
1 each medium red and green bell
    pepper, cored, seeded and cut
    into 1-inch-wide strips
½ cup Marsala or sweet vermouth
    (optional)
    Olive oil

To make polenta, bring chicken broth to a boil in large pot. Add polenta and cook at a gentle boil, stirring frequently, about 30 minutes. If polenta starts to stick and burn bottom of pot, add up to ½ cup water. During last 5 minutes of cooking, stir in corn and butter. Remove from heat; stir in Parmesan cheese. Transfer polenta into greased 13×9-inch baking pan; let cool until firm and set enough to cut. (Polenta can be prepared a day ahead and held in refrigerator.)

Prick each sausage in 4 or 5 places with fork. Place sausages, red onions and bell peppers in large shallow glass dish or large heavy plastic food storage bag. Pour Marsala over food; cover dish or close bag. Marinate in refrigerator up to 4 hours, turning sausages and vegetables several times. (If you don't wish to marinate sausages and vegetables in Marsala, just eliminate this step.)

Oil hot grid to help prevent sticking. Cut polenta into squares, then cut into triangles, if desired. Brush one side with oil. Grill polenta oil side down, on a covered grill, over medium **KINGSFORD®** Briquets, about 4 minutes until lightly toasted. Halfway through cooking time, brush top with oil, then turn and continue grilling. Move polenta to edge of grill to keep warm.

When coals are medium-low, drain sausages and vegetables from wine; discard wine. Grill sausages on covered grill, 15 to 20 minutes until cooked through, turning several times. After sausages have cooked 10 minutes, place vegetables in center of grid. Grill vegetables 10 to 12 minutes until tender, turning once or twice.

Makes 6 servings

Polska Kielbasa Simmered in Beer and Onions

4 tablespoons butter
4 onions, thinly sliced
1 pound HILLSHIRE FARM® Polska
    Kielbasa, diagonally sliced into
    ¼-inch pieces
1 bottle (12 ounces) beer

Melt butter in large skillet over medium heat; sauté onions 4 to 5 minutes. Add Polska Kielbasa; brown 3 to 4 minutes on each side. Pour beer into skillet; bring to a boil. Reduce heat and simmer, uncovered, 25 minutes. *Makes 4 to 6 servings*

Sausage, Peppers & Onions with Grilled Polenta

Poultry Perfection

Creole Chicken

1½ tablespoons vegetable oil
1 whole chicken, cut up, or 2 pounds
  chicken pieces
1½ tablespoons butter or margarine
1 medium onion, thinly sliced
2 teaspoons LAWRY'S® Garlic Powder
  with Parsley
1½ teaspoons LAWRY'S® Seasoned Salt
1 teaspoon LAWRY'S® Seasoned
  Pepper
1 can (8 ounces) tomato sauce
½ cup red wine
3 medium tomatoes, chopped
1 red bell pepper, sliced into strips
1 green bell pepper, sliced into strips
3 cups hot cooked rice

In large skillet, heat oil. Cook chicken over medium high heat until brown, about 5 minutes. Remove and set aside. In same skillet, melt butter; cook onion over medium high heat until tender. Add Garlic Powder with Parsley, Seasoned Salt and Seasoned Pepper. Return chicken pieces to skillet. Add remaining ingredients except rice. Cover and simmer over low heat 30 to 40 minutes until chicken is cooked. Serve over rice. *Makes 4 to 6 servings*

Turkey with Mustard Sauce

1 tablespoon butter or margarine
1 pound turkey cutlets
1 cup BIRDS EYE® frozen Mixed
  Vegetables
1 box (10 ounces) BIRDS EYE® frozen
  Pearl Onions in Cream Sauce
1 teaspoon spicy brown mustard

• In large nonstick skillet, melt butter over medium-high heat. Add turkey; cook until browned on both sides.

• Add mixed vegetables, onions with cream sauce and mustard; bring to boil. Reduce heat to medium-low; cover and simmer 6 to 8 minutes or until vegetables are tender and turkey is no longer pink in center. *Makes 4 servings*

Serving Suggestion: Serve with a fresh garden salad.

Prep Time: 5 minutes

Cook Time: 15 minutes

Creole Chicken

Chicken-Asparagus Casserole

2 teaspoons vegetable oil
1 cup seeded and chopped green
    and/or red bell peppers
1 medium onion, chopped
2 cloves garlic, minced
1 can (10¾ ounces) condensed
    cream of asparagus soup
2 eggs
1 container (8 ounces) ricotta cheese
2 cups (8 ounces) shredded Cheddar
    cheese, divided
1½ cups chopped cooked chicken
1 package (10 ounces) frozen
    chopped asparagus,* thawed and
    drained
8 ounces egg noodles, cooked
    Ground black pepper (optional)

*Or, substitute ½ pound fresh asparagus cut into
½-inch pieces. Bring 6 cups water to a boil over high
heat in large saucepan. Add fresh asparagus. Reduce
heat to medium. Cover and cook 5 to 8 minutes or
until crisp-tender. Drain.

1. Preheat oven to 350°F. Grease 13×9-
inch casserole; set aside.

2. Heat oil in small skillet over medium
heat. Add bell peppers, onion and garlic;
cook and stir until crisp-tender.

3. Mix soup, eggs, ricotta cheese and
1 cup Cheddar cheese in large bowl until
well blended. Add onion mixture, chicken,
asparagus and noodles; mix well. Season
with pepper, if desired.

4. Spread mixture evenly in prepared
casserole. Top with remaining 1 cup
Cheddar cheese.

5. Bake 30 minutes or until center is set
and cheese is bubbly. Let stand 5 minutes
before serving. Garnish as desired.
Makes 12 servings

Broiled Chicken with Honeyed Onion Sauce

2 pounds boneless skinless chicken
    thighs
4 teaspoons olive oil, divided
1 teaspoon paprika
1 teaspoon dried oregano leaves
1 teaspoon salt, divided
½ teaspoon ground cumin
¼ teaspoon black pepper
1 onion, sliced
2 cloves garlic, minced
¼ cup golden raisins
¼ cup honey
2 tablespoons lemon juice

1. Preheat broiler. Rub chicken with
2 teaspoons olive oil. Combine paprika,
oregano, ½ teaspoon salt, cumin and
pepper; rub mixture over chicken.

2. Place chicken on broiler pan. Broil about
6 inches from heat 5 minutes per side or
until chicken is no longer pink in center.

3. While chicken is cooking, heat
remaining 2 teaspoons oil in medium
nonstick skillet. Add onion and garlic; cook
about 8 minutes or until onion is dark
golden brown, stirring occasionally.

4. Stir in raisins, honey, lemon juice,
remaining ½ teaspoon salt and ¼ cup
water. Simmer, uncovered, until slightly
thickened. Spoon sauce over chicken.
Makes 4 servings

Serving Suggestion: Serve with a quick-
cooking rice pilaf and mixed green salad.

Prep and Cook Time: 28 minutes

Chicken-Asparagus Casserole

Chicken Cacciatore

1 tablespoon olive oil
1 broiler-fryer chicken (3 to 3½ pounds), cut into 8 pieces
4 ounces fresh mushrooms, finely chopped
1 medium onion, chopped
1 clove garlic, minced
½ cup dry white wine
1 tablespoon plus 1½ teaspoons white wine vinegar
½ cup chicken broth
1 teaspoon dried basil leaves, crushed
½ teaspoon dried marjoram leaves, crushed
½ teaspoon salt
⅛ teaspoon pepper
1 can (14½ ounces) whole tomatoes, undrained
8 Italian- or Greek-style black olives, halved, pitted
1 tablespoon chopped fresh parsley
Hot cooked pasta
Fresh marjoram leaves for garnish

Heat oil in large skillet over medium heat. Add as many chicken pieces in single layer without crowding to hot oil. Cook 8 minutes per side or until chicken is brown; remove chicken with slotted spatula to Dutch oven. Repeat with remaining chicken pieces.

Add mushrooms and onion to drippings remaining in skillet. Cook and stir over medium heat 5 minutes or until onion is soft. Add garlic; cook and stir 30 seconds. Add wine and vinegar; cook over medium-high heat 5 minutes or until liquid is almost evaporated. Stir in broth, basil, marjoram, salt and pepper. Remove from heat.

Press tomatoes and juice through sieve into onion mixture; discard seeds. Bring to a boil over medium-high heat; boil, uncovered, 2 minutes. Pour tomato-onion mixture over chicken. Bring to a boil; reduce heat to low. Cover and simmer 25 minutes or until chicken is tender and juices run clear when pierced with fork. Remove chicken with slotted spatula to heated serving dish; keep warm.

Bring tomato-onion sauce to a boil over medium-high heat; boil, uncovered, 5 minutes. Add olives and parsley to sauce; cook 1 minute more. Pour sauce over chicken and pasta. Garnish, if desired.
Makes 4 to 6 servings

Buying Onions

Onions are sold either in prepacked sacks or in bulk. When buying onions, choose those with short necks and dry papery outer skins. They should be firm and free from blemishes.

Chicken Cacciatore

Baked Chicken and Garlic Orzo

Nonstick cooking spray
4 chicken breast halves, skinned
¼ cup dry white wine
10 ounces uncooked orzo pasta
1 cup chopped onion
4 cloves garlic, minced
2 tablespoons chopped fresh parsley
1 teaspoon dried oregano leaves
1 can (about 14 ounces) fat-free reduced-sodium chicken broth
¼ cup water
Paprika
1 teaspoon lemon pepper
¼ teaspoon salt
2 teaspoons olive oil
1 lemon, cut into 8 wedges

1. Preheat oven to 350°F. Spray large nonstick skillet with cooking spray. Heat over high heat until hot. Add chicken breast halves. Cook, meat side down, 1 to 2 minutes or until lightly browned; set aside.

2. Reduce heat to medium-high; add wine. Stir with flat spatula, scraping brown bits from bottom of pan. Cook 30 seconds or until slightly reduced; set aside.

3. Spray 9-inch square baking pan with nonstick cooking spray. Add pasta, onion, garlic, parsley, oregano, chicken broth, water and wine mixture; stir. Place chicken breasts on top. Sprinkle lightly with paprika and lemon pepper. Bake, uncovered, 1 hour and 10 minutes. Remove chicken. Add salt and olive oil to baking pan; mix well. Place chicken on top. Serve with fresh lemon wedges.

Makes 4 servings

Chicken Scaparella

2 slices bacon, coarsely chopped
2 tablespoons FILIPPO BERIO® Olive Oil
1 large chicken breast, split
½ cup quartered mushrooms
1 small clove garlic, minced
1 cup plus 2 tablespoons chicken broth, divided
2 tablespoons red wine vinegar
8 small white onions, peeled
4 small new potatoes, cut into halves
½ teaspoon salt
⅛ teaspoon pepper
1 tablespoon all-purpose flour
Chopped fresh parsley

Cook bacon in skillet. Remove bacon with slotted spoon; set aside. Pour off drippings. Add oil and chicken. Brown well on all sides. Add mushrooms and garlic. Sauté several minutes, stirring occasionally. Add 1 cup broth, vinegar, onions, potatoes, salt and pepper. Cover and simmer 35 minutes until chicken and vegetables are tender.

To thicken sauce, dissolve flour in 2 tablespoons chicken broth. Stir into sauce. Cook, stirring, until thickened and smooth. Garnish with reserved bacon and parsley.

Makes 2 servings

Chicken Scaparella

Chicken Pot Pie

1½ pounds chicken pieces, skinned
1 cup chicken broth
½ teaspoon salt
¼ teaspoon black pepper
1 to 1½ cups reduced-fat (2%) milk
3 tablespoons margarine or butter
1 medium onion, chopped
1 cup sliced celery
⅓ cup all-purpose flour
2 cups frozen mixed vegetables
   (broccoli, carrots and cauliflower
   combination), thawed
½ teaspoon dried thyme leaves
1 tablespoon chopped fresh parsley
   or 1 teaspoon dried parsley
1 (9-inch) refrigerated pastry crust
1 egg, slightly beaten

Combine chicken, chicken broth, salt and pepper in large saucepan over medium-high heat. Bring to a boil. Reduce heat to low. Cover; simmer 30 minutes or until juices run clear.

Remove chicken and let cool. Pour remaining chicken broth mixture into glass measure. Let stand; spoon off fat. Add enough milk to broth mixture to equal 2½ cups. Remove chicken from bones and cut into ½-inch pieces.

Melt margarine in same saucepan over medium heat. Add onion and celery. Cook and stir 3 minutes. Stir in flour until well blended. Gradually stir in broth mixture. Cook, stirring constantly, until sauce thickens and boils. Add chicken, vegetables, thyme and parsley. Pour into 1½-quart deep casserole.

Preheat oven to 400°F. Roll out pastry 1 inch larger than diameter of casserole on lightly floured surface. Cut slits in pastry for venting air. Place pastry on top of casserole. Roll edges and cut away extra pastry; flute edges. Reroll scraps to cut into decorative designs. Place on top of pastry. Brush pastry with beaten egg. Bake about 30 minutes until crust is golden brown and filling is bubbling.

Makes about 6 cups or 4 servings

Southwest Turkey Tenderloin Stew

1 package (about 1½ pounds) turkey
   tenderloins, cut into ¾-inch
   pieces
1 tablespoon chili powder
1 teaspoon ground cumin
¾ teaspoon salt
1 red bell pepper, cut into ¾-inch
   pieces
1 green bell pepper, cut into ¾-inch
   pieces
¾ cup chopped red or yellow onion
3 cloves garlic, minced
1 can (15½ ounces) chili beans in
   spicy sauce, undrained
1 can (14½ ounces) chili-style stewed
   tomatoes, undrained
¾ cup prepared salsa or picante sauce
Fresh cilantro (optional)

SLOW COOKER DIRECTIONS
Place turkey in slow cooker. Sprinkle chili powder, cumin and salt over turkey; toss to coat. Add red bell pepper, green bell pepper, onion, garlic, beans, tomatoes and salsa. Mix well. Cover and cook on LOW 5 hours or until turkey is no longer pink in center and vegetables are crisp-tender. Ladle into bowls. Garnish with cilantro, if desired. *Makes 6 servings*

*Southwest Turkey
Tenderloin Stew*

Fish & Seafood

Seafood Paella

1 tablespoon olive oil
4 cloves garlic, minced
4½ cups finely chopped onions
2 cups uncooked long-grain white
    rice
2 cups clam juice
2 cups dry white wine
3 tablespoons fresh lemon juice
½ teaspoon paprika
¼ cup boiling water
½ teaspoon saffron or ground
    turmeric
1½ cups peeled and diced plum
    tomatoes
½ cup chopped fresh parsley
1 jar (8 ounces) roasted red peppers,
    drained, thinly sliced and divided
1 pound bay scallops
1½ cups frozen peas, thawed
10 clams, scrubbed
10 mussels, scrubbed
1 cup water
20 large shrimp (1 pound), shelled
    and deveined

Preheat oven to 375°F. Heat oil in large ovenproof skillet or paella pan over medium-low heat until hot. Add garlic and cook just until garlic sizzles. Add onions and rice; cook and stir 10 minutes or until onions are soft. Stir in clam juice, wine, lemon juice and paprika; mix well.

Combine boiling water and saffron in small bowl; stir until saffron is dissolved. Stir into onion mixture. Stir in tomatoes, parsley and half the red peppers. Bring to a boil over medium heat. Remove from heat; cover. Place on lowest shelf of oven. Bake 1 hour or until all liquid is absorbed. Remove from oven; stir in scallops and peas. Turn oven off; return paella to oven.

In Dutch oven, steam clams and mussels 4 to 6 minutes in 1 cup water, removing each as shell opens. (Discard any unopened clams or mussels.) Steam shrimp 2 to 3 minutes just until shrimp turn pink and opaque. Remove paella from oven and arrange clams, mussels and shrimp on top. Garnish with remaining red peppers. *Makes 10 servings*

Seafood Paella

Lemon Sesame Scallops

8 ounces whole wheat spaghetti
3 tablespoons sesame oil, divided
1 pound sea scallops
¼ cup chicken broth or clam juice
½ teaspoon grated lemon peel
3 tablespoons lemon juice
2 tablespoons oyster sauce
1 tablespoon soy sauce
1 tablespoon cornstarch
1 tablespoon vegetable oil
2 carrots, cut into julienne strips
1 yellow bell pepper, cut into thin
   strips
4 slices peeled fresh ginger
1 clove garlic, minced
6 ounces fresh snow peas, trimmed
   or 1 (6-ounce) package frozen
   snow peas, thawed
2 green onions, thinly sliced
1 tablespoon sesame seeds, toasted

Cook spaghetti according to package directions; drain. Place spaghetti in large bowl; toss with 2 tablespoons sesame oil. Cover to keep warm.

Rinse scallops and pat dry with paper towels; set aside. Combine broth, lemon peel, lemon juice, oyster sauce, soy sauce and cornstarch in 1-cup glass measure; set aside. Heat remaining 1 tablespoon sesame oil and vegetable oil in large skillet or wok over medium heat. Add carrots and bell pepper; stir-fry 4 to 5 minutes or until crisp-tender. Transfer to large bowl; set aside.

Add ginger and garlic to skillet. Stir-fry 1 minute over medium high-heat. Add scallops; stir-fry 1 minute. Add snow peas and onions; stir-fry 2 to 3 minutes or until peas turn bright green and scallops turn opaque. Remove slices of ginger; discard. Transfer scallop mixture to bowl with vegetable mixture, leaving any liquid in skillet.

Stir broth mixture; add to liquid in skillet. Cook and stir 5 minutes or until thickened. Return scallop mixture to skillet; cook 1 minute. Serve immediately over warm spaghetti; sprinkle with sesame seeds.

Makes 4 servings

Grilled Tuna with Salsa Salad

1 bag (16 ounces) BIRDS EYE® frozen
   Farm Fresh Mixtures Broccoli,
   Corn & Red Peppers
6 to 8 green onions, sliced
1 to 2 jalapeño peppers, finely
   chopped
1 can (14½ ounces) diced tomatoes
   with garlic and onion*
1 tablespoon, or to taste, lime juice
   or vinegar
4 tuna steaks, grilled as desired

*Or, substitute favorite seasoned diced tomatoes.

• In large saucepan, cook vegetables according to package directions; drain.

• In large bowl, combine vegetables, onions, peppers, tomatoes and lime juice. Let stand 15 minutes.

• Serve vegetable mixture over tuna.

Makes 4 servings

Prep Time: 5 minutes
Cook Time: 10 minutes

Lemon Sesame Scallops

Shrimp and Crab Enchiladas

1 package (1.42 ounces) LAWRY'S® Extra Rich & Thick Spaghetti Sauce Spices & Seasoning
1 can (28 ounces) whole tomatoes, cut up
1 can (4 ounces) diced green chiles
½ teaspoon ground cumin
1 tablespoon vegetable oil
1 onion, chopped
1 teaspoon LAWRY'S® Garlic Powder with Parsley
½ pound cooked medium shrimp, cut in half crosswise
½ pound lump crabmeat or imitation crab, shredded
¼ to ½ teaspoon hot pepper sauce
2 cups (8 ounces) grated Monterey Jack cheese, divided
6 flour tortillas

In medium saucepan, combine Extra Rich & Thick Spaghetti Sauce Spices & Seasonings, tomatoes, green chiles and cumin. Bring to a boil over medium high heat; reduce heat to low, cover and simmer 20 minutes, stirring occasionally. In medium skillet, heat oil. Cook onion with Garlic Powder with Parsley over medium high heat until onion is tender. Remove from heat; add shrimp, crab, hot pepper sauce and 1 cup cheese. Place ½ cup mixture on each tortilla. Roll up securely. In 12×8×2-inch baking dish, pour ½ cup prepared sauce. Place tortillas seam-side down in dish. Cover with remaining sauce. Bake in 375°F oven 15 to 20 minutes. Top with remaining 1 cup cheese; bake an additional 15 minutes or until cheese is melted.

Makes 6 servings

Serving Suggestion: Top with guacamole and dairy sour cream and serve with Mexican rice.

Blackened Snapper with Red Onion Salsa

Cajun Seasoning Mix (recipe follows)
Red Onion Salsa (recipe follows)
4 red snapper fillets (about 6 ounces each)
2 tablespoons butter

Prepare Cajun Seasoning Mix and Red Onion Salsa; set aside. Rinse red snapper and pat dry with paper towels. Sprinkle with Cajun Seasoning Mix. Heat large, heavy skillet over high heat until very hot. Add butter and swirl skillet to coat bottom. When butter no longer bubbles, place fish in pan. Cook fish 6 to 8 minutes or until surface is very brown and fish flakes easily when tested with fork, turning halfway through cooking. Serve with Red Onion Salsa. *Makes 4 servings*

Cajun Seasoning Mix: Combine 2 tablespoons salt, 1 tablespoon paprika, 1½ teaspoons garlic powder, 1 teaspoon *each* onion powder and ground red pepper, ½ teaspoon ground white pepper, ½ teaspoon black pepper, ½ teaspoon dried thyme leaves and ½ teaspoon dried oregano leaves in small bowl. Set aside.

Red Onion Salsa

1 tablespoon vegetable oil
1 large red onion, chopped
1 clove garlic, minced
½ cup chicken broth
¼ cup dry red wine
¼ teaspoon dried thyme leaves
Salt and black pepper to taste

Heat oil in small saucepan over medium-high heat. Add onion; cover and cook 5 minutes. Add garlic; cook 1 minute. Add remaining ingredients; cover and cook 10 minutes. Uncover; cook until liquid reduces to ¼ cup.

Brazilian Corn and Shrimp Moqueca Casserole

2 tablespoons olive oil
½ cup chopped onion
¼ cup chopped green bell pepper
¼ cup tomato sauce
2 tablespoons chopped parsley
½ teaspoon TABASCO® brand Pepper Sauce
1 pound medium cooked shrimp
  Salt to taste
2 tablespoons all-purpose flour
1 cup milk
1 can (16 ounces) cream-style corn
  Grated Parmesan cheese

In large oven-proof skillet over medium-high heat, heat oil. Add onion, bell pepper, tomato sauce, parsley and TABASCO® Sauce and cook, stirring occasionally, for 5 minutes. Add shrimp and salt. Cover and reduce heat to low, and simmer for 2 to 3 minutes. Preheat oven to 375°F. Sprinkle flour over shrimp mixture; stir. Add milk gradually, stirring after each addition. Cook over medium heat until mixture thickens. Remove from heat. Pour corn over mixture; do not stir. Sprinkle with Parmesan cheese. Bake for 30 minutes or until browned.

Makes 4 servings

Grilled Salmon Fillets, Asparagus and Onions

½ teaspoon paprika, preferably sweet Hungarian
6 salmon fillets (6 to 8 ounces *each*)
⅓ cup bottled honey-Dijon marinade *or* barbecue sauce
1 bunch (about 1 pound) fresh asparagus spears, ends trimmed
1 large red or sweet onion, cut into ¼-inch slices
1 tablespoon olive oil

1. Prepare grill for grilling. Sprinkle paprika evenly over salmon fillets. Brush marinade over salmon; let stand at room temperature 15 minutes.

2. Brush asparagus and onion slices with olive oil; season with salt and pepper.

3. Place salmon, skin side down, in center of grid over medium coals. Arrange asparagus spears and onion slices around salmon on grid. Grill salmon and vegetables over covered grill 5 minutes. Turn asparagus and onion slices. Grill 5 to 6 minutes more or until salmon flakes easily when tested with a fork and vegetables are crisp-tender. Separate onion slices into rings; arrange over asparagus.

Makes 6 servings

Prep and Cook Time: 26 minutes

Pasta with Shrimp, Broccoli and Red Pepper

8 ounces uncooked capellini, linguine or thin spaghetti
2 tablespoons FILIPPO BERIO® Olive Oil
1 medium onion, finely chopped
1 clove garlic, minced
1 bunch fresh broccoli, trimmed and separated into florets
½ cup chicken broth
8 ounces cooked peeled and deveined shrimp
1 red bell pepper, seeded and thinly sliced
2 tablespoons chopped fresh Italian parsley
1 fresh jalapeño pepper, seeded and minced
Salt and freshly ground black pepper

Cook pasta according to package directions until al dente (tender but still firm). Drain. Meanwhile, in large saucepan or Dutch oven, heat olive oil over medium heat until hot. Add onion and garlic; cook and stir 5 minutes or until onion is tender. Add broccoli and broth. Cover; reduce heat to low. Simmer 8 to 10 minutes or until broccoli is tender-crisp. Add shrimp, bell pepper, parsley and jalapeño pepper; stir occasionally until heated through. Add pasta to broccoli mixture; toss until lightly coated. Season to taste with salt and black pepper. *Makes 4 servings*

Lemon-Garlic Shrimp

1 package (6.2 ounces) RICE-A-RONI® With ⅓ Less Salt Broccoli Au Gratin
1 tablespoon margarine or butter
1 pound raw medium shrimp, shelled and deveined or large scallops, cut into halves
1 medium red or green bell pepper, cut into short thin strips
2 cloves garlic, minced
½ teaspoon Italian seasoning
½ cup reduced-sodium or regular chicken broth
1 tablespoon lemon juice
1 tablespoon cornstarch
3 medium green onions, cut into ½-inch pieces
1 teaspoon grated lemon peel

1. Prepare Rice-A-Roni® Mix as package directs.

2. While Rice-A-Roni® is simmering, heat margarine in second large skillet or wok over medium-high heat. Add shrimp, red pepper, garlic and Italian seasoning. Stir-fry 3 to 4 minutes or until shrimp is opaque.

3. Combine chicken broth, lemon juice and cornstarch, mixing until smooth. Add broth mixture and onions to skillet. Stir-fry 2 to 3 minutes or until sauce thickens.

4. Stir ½ teaspoon lemon peel into rice. Serve rice topped with shrimp mixture; sprinkle with remaining ½ teaspoon lemon peel. *Makes 4 servings*

Lemon-Garlic Shrimp

Seafood Stew

2 tablespoons butter or margarine
1 cup chopped onion
1 cup green bell pepper strips
1 teaspoon dried dill weed
  Dash ground red pepper
1 can (14½ ounces) diced tomatoes,
  undrained
½ cup white wine
2 tablespoons lime juice
8 ounces swordfish steak, cut into
  1-inch cubes
8 ounces bay or sea scallops, cut into
  quarters
1 bottle (8 ounces) clam juice
2 tablespoons cornstarch
2 cups frozen diced potatoes,
  thawed and drained
8 ounces frozen cooked medium
  shrimp, thawed and drained
½ cup whipping cream

1. Melt butter in Dutch oven over medium-high heat. Add onion, bell pepper, dill weed and red pepper; cook and stir 5 minutes or until vegetables are tender.

2. Reduce heat to medium. Add tomatoes with juice, wine and lime juice; bring to a boil. Add swordfish and scallops; cook and stir 2 minutes.

3. Combine clam juice and cornstarch in small bowl; stir until smooth.

4. Increase heat to high. Add potatoes, shrimp, whipping cream and clam juice mixture; bring to a boil. Season to taste with salt and black pepper.

Makes 6 servings

Serving Suggestion: For a special touch, garnish stew with fresh lemon wedges and basil leaves.

Prep and Cook Time: 20 minutes

Easy Tuna & Pasta Pot Pie

1 tablespoon margarine or butter
1 large onion, chopped
1½ cups cooked small shell pasta or
  elbow macaroni
1 can (10¾ ounces) condensed
  cream of celery or mushroom
  soup, undiluted
1 cup frozen peas, thawed
1 can (6 ounces) tuna in water,
  drained and broken into pieces
½ cup sour cream
½ teaspoon dried dill weed
¼ teaspoon salt
1 package (7½ ounces) refrigerated
  buttermilk or country biscuits

1. Preheat oven to 400°F. Melt margarine in medium ovenproof skillet over medium heat. Add onion; cook 5 minutes, stirring occasionally.

2. Stir in pasta, soup, peas, tuna, sour cream, dill and salt; mix well. Cook 3 minutes or until hot. Press mixture down in skillet to form even layer.

3. Unwrap biscuit dough; arrange individual biscuits over tuna mixture. Bake 15 minutes or until biscuits are golden brown and tuna mixture is bubbly.

Makes 5 servings

Prep and Cook Time: 28 minutes

Easy Tuna & Pasta Pot Pie

Soups & Salads

Oniony Mushroom Soup

2 cans (10¾ ounces each) condensed golden mushroom soup
1 can (13¾ ounces) reduced-sodium beef broth
1⅓ cups FRENCH'S® French Fried Onions, divided
½ cup water
⅓ cup dry sherry wine
4 slices French bread, cut ½ inch thick
1 tablespoon olive oil
1 clove garlic, finely minced
1 cup (4 ounces) shredded Swiss cheese

Combine mushroom soup, beef broth, *1 cup* French Fried Onions, water and sherry in large saucepan. Bring to a boil over medium-high heat, stirring often. Reduce heat to low. Simmer 15 minutes, stirring occasionally.

Preheat broiler. Place bread on baking sheet. Combine oil and garlic; brush over both sides of bread. Broil until toasted and crisp, turning once.

Ladle soup into 4 broiler-safe bowls. Place 1 slice of bread in each bowl. Sprinkle evenly with cheese and remaining *⅓ cup* onions. Place bowls on baking sheet. Place under broiler about 1 minute or until cheese is melted and onions are golden.

Makes 4 servings

Greek Pasta Salad

½ pound extra-lean (90% lean) ground beef
⅓ cup chopped fresh mint *or* 2 tablespoons dried mint leaves
1 clove garlic, minced
1¾ cups (about 6 ounces) small shell macaroni, cooked
10 cherry tomatoes, quartered
2 ounces feta cheese, crumbled
½ red bell pepper, chopped
½ red onion, cut into rings
¼ cup reduced-calorie Italian dressing
2 tablespoons lemon juice
Salt and freshly ground black pepper
Lettuce leaves

Brown ground beef in medium skillet. Drain. Add mint and garlic; cook 2 minutes, stirring constantly.

Spoon ground beef mixture into large bowl. Stir in pasta, tomatoes, cheese, red bell pepper and onion. Add dressing and lemon juice; toss lightly. Season with salt and black pepper to taste. Serve on lettuce-covered salad plates.

Makes 4 servings

Note: Salad can be made up to 4 hours in advance.

Oniony Mushroom Soup

Pasta e Fagioli

2 tablespoons olive oil
1 cup chopped onion
3 cloves garlic, minced
2 cans (14½ ounces *each*) Italian-style
    stewed tomatoes, undrained
3 cups ⅓-less-salt chicken broth
1 can (about 15 ounces) cannellini
    beans (white kidney beans),
    undrained*
¼ cup chopped fresh Italian parsley
1 teaspoon dried basil leaves
¼ teaspoon black pepper
4 ounces uncooked small shell pasta

*One can (about 15 ounces) Great Northern beans,
undrained, may be substituted for cannellini beans.*

1. Heat oil in 4-quart Dutch oven over
medium heat until hot; add onion and
garlic. Cook and stir 5 minutes or until
onion is tender.

2. Stir tomatoes with liquid, chicken broth,
beans with liquid, parsley, basil and
pepper into Dutch oven; bring to a boil
over high heat, stirring occasionally.
Reduce heat to low. Simmer, covered,
10 minutes.

3. Add pasta to Dutch oven. Simmer,
covered, 10 to 12 minutes or until pasta is
just tender. Serve immediately. Garnish as
desired.   *Makes 8 servings*

Classic French Onion Soup

¼ cup butter
3 large yellow onions, sliced
1 cup dry white wine
3 cans (about 14 ounces *each*) beef
    or chicken broth
½ teaspoon dried thyme
½ teaspoon salt
1 teaspoon Worcestershire sauce
1 loaf French bread, sliced and
    toasted
4 ounces shredded Swiss cheese
    Fresh thyme for garnish

SLOW COOKER DIRECTIONS
Melt butter in large skillet over high heat.
Add onions, cook and stir 15 minutes or
until onions are soft and lightly browned.
Stir in wine.

Combine onion mixture, beef broth,
thyme, salt and Worcestershire in slow
cooker. Cover and cook on LOW 4 to
4½ hours. Ladle soup into 4 individual
bowls; top with bread slice and cheese.
Garnish with fresh thyme, if desired.
                    Makes 4 servings

Pasta e Fagioli

Pasta Pesto Salad

PASTA SALAD
8 ounces three-color rotini pasta
3 small bell peppers (green, red and yellow), seeded and cut into thin strips
1 pint cherry tomatoes, stemmed and halved (2 cups)
6 ounces (1 block) ALPINE LACE® Fat Free Pasteurized Process Skim Milk Cheese Product—For Mozzarella Lovers, cut into ½-inch cubes (1½ cups)
1 cup thin carrot circles
1 cup thin strips red onion
1 cup slivered fresh basil leaves

SPICY DRESSING
½ cup (2 ounces) shredded ALPINE LACE® Fat Free Pasteurized Process Skim Milk Cheese Product—For Parmesan Lovers
⅓ cup firmly packed fresh parsley
⅓ cup extra virgin olive oil
⅓ cup red wine vinegar
2 large cloves garlic
1 tablespoon whole-grain Dijon mustard
¾ teaspoon black pepper
½ teaspoon salt

1. To make the Pasta Salad: Cook the pasta according to package directions until al dente. Drain in a colander, rinse under cold water and drain again. Place the pasta in a large shallow pasta bowl and toss with the remaining salad ingredients.

2. To make the Spicy Dressing: In a food processor or blender, process all of the dressing ingredients for 30 seconds or until well blended.

3. Drizzle the dressing on the salad and toss to mix thoroughly. Cover with plastic wrap and refrigerate for 1 hour so that the flavors can blend, or let stand at room temperature for 1 hour.

Makes 6 main-dish servings

Vegetable Beef Noodle Soup

8 ounces beef stew meat, cut into ½-inch pieces
¾ cup unpeeled cubed potato (1 medium)
½ cup sliced carrot
1 tablespoon balsamic vinegar
¾ teaspoon dried thyme leaves
¼ teaspoon black pepper
2½ cups fat-free reduced-sodium beef broth
1 cup water
¼ cup prepared chili sauce or ketchup
2 ounces uncooked thin egg noodles
¾ cup jarred or canned pearl onions, rinsed and drained
¼ cup frozen peas

1. Heat large saucepan over high heat until hot; add beef. Cook 3 minutes or until browned on all sides, stirring occasionally. Remove from pan.

2. Cook potato, carrot, vinegar, thyme and pepper 3 minutes in same saucepan over medium heat. Add beef broth, water and chili sauce. Bring to a boil over medium-high; add beef. Reduce heat to medium-low; simmer, covered, 30 minutes or until meat is almost fork tender.

3. Bring beef mixture to a boil over medium-high heat. Add pasta; cook, covered, 7 to 10 minutes or until pasta is tender, stirring occasionally. Add onions and peas; heat 1 minute. Serve immediately.

Makes 6 (1½-cup) servings

Pasta Pesto Salad

Oniony Bacon 'n' Egg Salad

1⅓ cups FRENCH'S® French Fried Onions
8 hard-cooked eggs, chopped
6 strips cooked bacon, chopped
3 plum tomatoes, seeded and chopped (1 cup chopped)
1 rib celery, finely chopped
½ cup low-fat mayonnaise
1 tablespoon FRENCH'S® Deli Brown Mustard
6 pita bread rounds, split

Place French Fried Onions in medium microwavable bowl. Microwave on HIGH 1 minute or until golden. Combine onions, eggs, bacon, tomatoes, celery, mayonnaise and mustard in large bowl. Mix just until eggs are moistened. Spoon into pita bread rounds.

Makes 6 to 8 servings

Tip: Spoon salad into baked pastry shells or into cooked new potato shells and serve as an appetizer.

Prep Time: 30 minutes

Cook Time: 1 minute

Cheesy Onion Soup

2 large onions, thinly sliced
1 clove garlic, minced
¼ cup butter
2 cups tomato juice
2⅔ cups beef broth
½ cup salsa
1 cup unseasoned croutons
1 cup (4 ounces) shredded Swiss cheese
Additional salsa for serving

1. Cook onions, garlic and butter in 3-quart saucepan over medium-low heat 20 minutes or until onions are tender and golden brown.

2. Stir in tomato juice, broth and ½ cup salsa. Bring to a boil over medium-high heat. Reduce heat to low. Simmer, uncovered, 20 minutes.

3. Ladle soup into bowls and sprinkle with croutons and cheese. Serve with additional salsa. *Makes 6 servings*

ONION TIP

Since 1982, onion consumption has risen over 50%! Onions provide the perfect way to add flavor to any dish.

Cheesy Onion Soup

Corn and Onion Chowder

¼ pound uncooked bacon, chopped
2 medium potatoes (¾ pound),
    peeled and cut into ¼-inch cubes
1⅓ cups FRENCH'S® French Fried
    Onions, divided
½ cup chopped celery
1 tablespoon fresh thyme *or*
    ¾ teaspoon dried thyme leaves
1 bay leaf
1½ cups water
2 cans (15 ounces each) cream-style
    corn, undrained
1½ cups milk
½ teaspoon salt
¼ teaspoon ground white or black
    pepper

Cook and stir bacon in large saucepan over medium-high heat until crisp and browned. Remove with slotted spoon to paper towel. Pour off all but 1 tablespoon drippings.

Add potatoes, ⅔ *cup* French Fried Onions, celery, thyme and bay leaf to saucepan. Stir in water. Bring to a boil over medium-high heat. Reduce heat to low. Cover; simmer 10 to 12 minutes or until potatoes are fork-tender, stirring occasionally.

Stir in corn, milk, salt, pepper and reserved bacon. Cook until heated through. *Do not boil.* Discard bay leaf. Ladle into individual soup bowls. Sprinkle with remaining ⅔ *cup* onions.   *Makes 6 to 8 servings*

Prep Time: 20 minutes
Cook Time: 20 minutes

Ravioli Soup

1 package (9 ounces) fresh or frozen
    cheese ravioli or tortellini
¾ pound hot Italian sausage,
    crumbled
1 can (14½ ounces) DEL MONTE®
    Italian Recipe Stewed Tomatoes
1 can (14 ounces) beef broth
1 can (14½ ounces) DEL MONTE® Cut
    Green Italian Beans, drained
2 green onions, sliced

1. Cook pasta according to package directions; drain.

2. Meanwhile, cook sausage in 5-quart pot over medium-high heat until no longer pink; drain. Add tomatoes, broth and 1¾ cups water; bring to boil.

3. Reduce heat to low; stir in pasta, green beans and green onions. Simmer until heated through. Season with pepper and sprinkle with grated Parmesan cheese, if desired.   *Makes 4 servings*

Prep and Cook Time: 15 minutes

Ravioli Soup

Thai Chicken Broccoli Salad

4 ounces uncooked linguine
½ pound boneless skinless chicken
    breasts, cut into 2×½-inch pieces
2 cups broccoli florets
⅔ cup chopped red bell pepper
6 green onions, sliced diagonally into
    1-inch pieces
¼ cup reduced-fat creamy peanut
    butter
2 tablespoons reduced-sodium soy
    sauce
2 teaspoons Oriental sesame oil
½ teaspoon red pepper flakes
⅛ teaspoon garlic powder
¼ cup unsalted peanuts, chopped

1. Cook pasta according to package directions, omitting salt. Drain.

2. Spray large nonstick skillet with nonstick cooking spray; heat over medium-high heat until hot. Add chicken; stir-fry 5 minutes or until chicken is no longer pink. Remove chicken from skillet.

3. Add broccoli and 2 tablespoons cold water to skillet. Cook, covered, 2 minutes. Uncover; cook and stir 2 minutes or until broccoli is crisp-tender. Remove broccoli from skillet. Combine pasta, chicken, broccoli, bell pepper and onions in large bowl.

4. Combine peanut butter, 2 tablespoons hot water, soy sauce, oil, red pepper and garlic powder in small bowl until well blended. Drizzle over pasta mixture; toss to coat. Top with peanuts before serving.

Makes 4 servings

Onion Soup with Pasta

3 cups sliced onions
3 cloves garlic, minced
½ teaspoon sugar
2 cans (14½ ounces *each*) reduced-
    sodium beef broth
½ cup uncooked small pasta stars
2 tablespoons dry sherry
¼ teaspoon salt
⅛ teaspoon black pepper
    Grated Parmesan cheese

1. Spray large saucepan with nonstick cooking spray; heat over medium heat until hot. Add onions and garlic. Cook, covered, 5 to 8 minutes or until onions are wilted. Stir in sugar; cook about 15 minutes or until onion mixture is very soft and browned.

2. Add broth to saucepan; bring to a boil. Add pasta and simmer, uncovered, 6 to 8 minutes or until tender. Stir in sherry, salt and pepper. Ladle soup into bowls; sprinkle lightly with Parmesan cheese.

Makes 4 servings

Onion Soup with Pasta

Savory Sides

Oven Roasted Potatoes and Onions with Herbs

3 pounds red potatoes, cut into
    1½-inch cubes
1 large sweet onion, such as Vidalia
    or Walla Walla, coarsely chopped
3 tablespoons olive oil
2 tablespoons butter, melted or
    bacon drippings
3 cloves garlic, minced
¾ teaspoon salt
¾ teaspoon coarsely ground black
    pepper
⅓ cup packed chopped mixed fresh
    herbs, such as basil, chives,
    parsley, oregano, rosemary, sage,
    tarragon and thyme

1. Preheat oven to 450°F.

2. Arrange potatoes and onion in large shallow roasting pan.

3. Combine oil, butter, garlic, salt and pepper in small bowl. Drizzle over potatoes and onion; toss well to combine.

4. Bake 30 minutes. Stir and bake 10 minutes more. Add herbs; toss well. Continue baking 10 to 15 minutes or until vegetables are tender and browned. Transfer to serving bowl. Garnish with fresh rosemary, if desired.

Makes 6 servings

Oven-Fried Tex-Mex Onion Rings

½ cup plain dry bread crumbs
⅓ cup yellow cornmeal
1½ teaspoons chili powder
⅛ to ¼ teaspoon ground red pepper
⅛ teaspoon salt
1 tablespoon plus 1½ teaspoons
    margarine, melted
2 medium onions (about 10 ounces),
    sliced ⅜ inch thick
2 egg whites

1. Preheat oven to 450°F. Spray large nonstick baking sheet with nonstick cooking spray; set aside.

2. Combine bread crumbs, cornmeal, chili powder, pepper and salt in medium shallow dish; mix well. Stir in margarine and 1 teaspoon water.

3. Separate onion slices into rings. Place egg whites in large bowl; beat lightly. Add onions; toss lightly to coat evenly. Transfer to bread crumb mixture; toss to coat evenly. Place in single layer on prepared baking sheet.

4. Bake 12 to 15 minutes or until onions are tender and coating is crisp.

Makes 6 servings

*Oven Roasted Potatoes and
Onions with Herbs*

Original Green Bean Casserole

1 can (10¾ ounces) condensed
  cream of mushroom soup
¾ cup milk
⅛ teaspoon ground black pepper
2 packages (9 ounces each) frozen
  cut green beans, thawed and
  drained *or* 2 cans (14.5 ounces
  each) cut green beans, drained
1⅓ cups FRENCH'S® French Fried
  Onions, divided

Preheat oven to 350°F. Combine soup, milk and ground pepper in 1½-quart casserole; stir until well blended. Stir in beans and ⅔ *cup* French Fried Onions.

Bake, uncovered, 30 minutes or until hot. Stir; sprinkle with remaining ⅔ *cup* onions. Bake 5 minutes or until onions are golden.

Makes 6 servings

Microwave Directions: Prepare green bean mixture as above; pour into 1½-quart microwave-safe casserole. Cook, covered, on HIGH 8 to 10 minutes or until heated through. Stir beans halfway through cooking time. Top with remaining onions; cook, uncovered, 1 minute. Let stand 5 minutes.

Prep Time: 5 minutes
Cook Time: 35 minutes

Old-Fashioned Onion Rings

½ cup buttermilk
½ cup prepared Ranch dressing
2 large onions, sliced ½-inch thick
  and separated into rings
  WESSON® Vegetable or Canola Oil
2 cups self-rising flour
2 teaspoons garlic salt
2 teaspoons lemon pepper
½ teaspoon cayenne pepper
2 eggs, slightly beaten with
  2 tablespoons water

In a large bowl, combine buttermilk and Ranch dressing; blend well. Add onions and toss until well coated. Cover; refrigerate at least 1 hour or overnight. Fill a large deep-fry pot or electric skillet to no more than half its depth with Wesson® Oil. Heat oil between 325°F to 350°F. In a large bowl, combine flour, garlic salt, lemon pepper and cayenne pepper; blend well. Working in small batches, place onion rings in flour mixture; coat well. Remove; dip into egg mixture. Return rings to flour mixture; coat well. Lightly shake off excess flour; fry until golden brown. Drain on paper towels. Sprinkle with additional garlic salt, if desired.

Makes 4 servings

Old-Fashioned Onion Rings

Buffalo Chili Onions

½ cup FRANK'S® REDHOT® Hot Sauce
½ cup (1 stick) butter or margarine,
   melted or olive oil
¼ cup chili sauce
1 tablespoon chili powder
4 large sweet onions, cut into
   ½-inch-thick slices

Whisk together REDHOT sauce, butter, chili sauce and chili powder in medium bowl until blended; brush on onion slices.

Place onions on grid. Grill over medium-high coals 10 minutes or until tender, turning and basting often with chili mixture. Serve warm.

Makes 6 side-dish servings

Tip: Onions may be prepared ahead and grilled just before serving.

Prep Time: 10 minutes

Cook Time: 10 minutes

Country Corn Bake

2 cans (11 ounces each) Mexican-
   style corn, drained*
1 can (10¾ ounces) condensed
   cream of potato soup
½ cup milk
½ cup thinly sliced celery
1⅓ cups FRENCH'S® French Fried
   Onions, divided
½ cup (2 ounces) shredded Cheddar
   cheese
2 tablespoons bacon bits**

Or, substitute 1 bag (16 ounces) frozen kernel corn, thawed and drained.

**Or, substitute 2 slices crumbled, cooked bacon.*

Preheat oven to 375°F. Combine corn, soup, milk, celery, ⅔ cup French Fried Onions, cheese and bacon bits in large bowl. Spoon mixture into 2-quart square baking dish. Cover; bake 30 minutes or until hot and bubbly. Stir; sprinkle with remaining ⅔ cup onions. Bake, uncovered, 3 minutes or until onions are golden.

Makes 4 to 6 servings

Prep Time: 10 minutes

Cook Time: 33 minutes

Roasted Onions

2 packages (20 ounces each) frozen
   baby onions
4 teaspoons brown sugar
1 teaspoon LAWRY'S® Seasoned Salt
   Dash LAWRY'S® Seasoned Pepper
2 tablespoons LAWRY'S® Au Jus
   Gravy Mix (dry mix)
½ cup water
½ cup dry white wine
3 tablespoons butter
2 tablespoons lemon juice
2 tablespoons chopped parsley
   (garnish)

In 2-quart baking dish, place onions and remaining ingredients except butter, lemon juice and parsley. Blend well; dot with butter. Cover and bake in 375°F oven 45 minutes; uncover and bake 15 to 20 minutes until top is glazed. Add lemon juice.

Makes 8 servings

Presentation: Sprinkle with chopped parsley before serving.

Buffalo Chili Onions

Brown Rice and Green Onion Pilaf

 2 tablespoons FILIPPO BERIO® Olive
　Oil
 ¾ cup chopped green onions, white
　part and about 2 inches of green
　part
 1 cup uncooked brown rice
 2½ cups chicken broth, defatted (see
　note) or water
 ½ teaspoon salt
　Additional green onion, green part
　sliced into matchstick-size strips
　(optional)

In heavy medium saucepan, heat olive oil over medium heat until hot. Add chopped green onions; cook and stir 3 to 4 minutes or until wilted. Add rice; cook and stir 3 to 4 minutes to coat rice with oil. Add chicken broth and salt; stir well. Bring to a boil. Cover; reduce heat to low and simmer 40 minutes or until rice is tender and liquid is absorbed. Garnish with additional green onion, if desired.

Makes 4 to 5 servings

Note: To defat chicken broth, refrigerate can of broth for at least 1 hour. Open can; use a spoon to lift out any solid fat floating on surface of broth.

Oven-Roasted Peppers and Onions

　Olive oil-flavored nonstick cooking
　spray
 2 medium green bell peppers
 2 medium red bell peppers
 2 medium yellow bell peppers
 4 small onions
 1 teaspoon Italian herb blend
 ½ teaspoon dried basil leaves
 ¼ teaspoon ground cumin

1. Preheat oven to 375°F. Spray 15×10-inch jelly-roll pan with cooking spray. Cut bell peppers into 1½-inch pieces. Cut onions into quarters. Place vegetables on prepared pan. Spray vegetables with cooking spray. Bake 20 minutes; stir. Sprinkle with herb blend, basil and cumin.

2. Increase oven temperature to 425°F. Bake 20 minutes or until edges are darkened and vegetables are crisp-tender.

Makes 6 servings

CUTTING NEWS

When cutting onions, be sure to use a sharp, stainless steel knife. Pure carbon steel will tend to discolor the onions. Don't chop onions in a food processor because it tends to make them mushy. It is okay to use a food processor for grating onions.

Oven-Roasted Peppers and Onions

Savory Sides

Onions Baked in Their Papers

4 medium-sized yellow onions (about
    2½ inches in diameter)*
1½ teaspoons mixed herbs such as
    dried thyme, sage and tarragon
    leaves, crushed
1 teaspoon sugar
½ teaspoon salt
    Dash red pepper flakes
¼ cup butter or margarine, melted
½ cup fresh bread crumbs
    Fresh tarragon sprigs, yellow
    squash strips, red bell pepper
    strips and chives for garnish

Choose onions with skins intact.

1. Preheat oven to 400°F. Line square
baking pan with foil; set aside. Slice off
stem and root ends of onions.

2. Cut 1½×1½-inch cone-shaped
indentation in the top of each onion with
paring knife. Set onions in prepared pan
cut side up.

3. Stir herbs, sugar, salt and red pepper
into melted butter. Add bread crumbs;
mix until blended. Spoon equal amounts
of crumb mixture into indentations.

4. Bake about 1 hour or until fork-tender.
Garnish, if desired. Serve immediately.
            Makes 4 side-dish servings

Tip: Onions make people cry because they
contain an enzyme called alliinase. When
this enzyme is exposed to air, it bonds
with sulphur, which stimulates tear ducts.
To minimize crying, chill onions before
slicing or run water over them before
cutting.

Creamed Pearl Onions

1 pint pearl onions (about
    10 ounces)
2 tablespoons butter or margarine
2 tablespoons all-purpose flour
1 cup half-and-half
¼ teaspoon *each* salt and pepper
¼ cup dry bread crumbs
    Red onion slices and fresh sage
    leaves for garnish

1. To peel onions easily, blanch onions
first. Cut stem end off onion; squeeze
onion between thumb and forefinger to
separate from its skin.

2. Place peeled onions in large saucepan
with ½ inch of water; cover. Bring to a boil
over high heat; reduce heat to medium-
low. Simmer 15 to 20 minutes until
fork-tender. Drain; set aside.

3. To make cream sauce, melt butter in
small saucepan over medium heat. Blend
in flour with wire whisk. Heat until mixture
bubbles. Whisk in half-and-half. Cook until
mixture thickens, whisking constantly. Add
salt and pepper. Stir in cooked onions.
Transfer creamed onions to warm serving
bowl. Sprinkle with dry bread crumbs.
Garnish, if desired. Serve immediately.
            Makes 4 side-dish servings